YOUR SPOUSE IS NOT
YOUR PROBLEM

Real Solutions for Real People

Dr. Tony and Kim Moore
The Center on Christian Relationships

RADICAL LOVE PUBLISHING
1870 South Lee Court
Buford, Georgia 30518
1-866-RADLOVE
www.radicallove.org

ISBN: 978-0-9786945-2-4

To all who have and continue to believe our message from God. You inspire us to run the race to which we have been assigned with grace and patience. Our heart is filled with appreciation for your contribution to our lives.

ACKNOWLEDGMENTS

We are grateful to Bishop Dale Bronner, Word of Faith Family Cathedral who believed in the very beginning: and not only believed, but spoke and gave resources to perform the work given us.

We appreciate The Radical Love Alumni Association whose desire to use this book in small groups, prompted this revision and the creation of an accompanying study guide.

Cover Design by:
Ibiyomi Jegede, IJ Creatives
www.ijcreatives.com

Table of Contents

INTRODUCTION

TODAY, there is general consensus that marriage, known as one man and one woman, is being attacked. All life is based on relationship. And second only to our relationship with God, the relationship most responsible for reproducing and maintaining organized civilization is marriage. Marriage results in families, churches, communities and countries. As men and women in marriage go, so goes our economic, political and social structure.

For the past fifty plus years, we have learned about our roles, responsibilities and needs as men and women, husbands and wives. Yet, the divorce rate continues unabated and cohabitation is at an all time high. The increase in dual income households requires many couples to re-evaluate previously assigned roles and responsibilities. And then there is the added dynamic of wives that earn more than their husbands.

So we made a choice. We will not echo the past fifty years of instruction, but rather focus on the next fifty years.

Couples today need principles that are impervious to the ever-changing variables that impact their marriage. One income, two income, one career, two careers, no children, many children, blended families, biological families, a lot of money, a little money, health, sickness, faithfulness, unfaithfulness and all of the other changing conditions we experience in life must not alter our response to marriage.

Newsflash: Marriage is perfect! It has no flaws. We cannot modify it, improve it, or work on it! You're fired! So stop trying! Moreover, did you ever consider that marriage, by design, does the same thing to all that dare to enter it? It blesses, breaks and serves every bride and groom. These three experiences occur over and over again as each spouse yields to God. We call these stages the ideal, the ordeal and real deal.

Among professional athletes and entertainers, only 2 out of 10 couples make it to the third stage, 3 out of 10 African American couples and 1 out of 2 European American couples make it. Most abort the process somewhere in the ordeal phase.

This is because marriage is heart work. Marriage is the process of developing unconditional love—the very nature of God. I John 4:8 and Romans 5:5 tell us that God is love and that His love has been poured out into our hearts by the Holy Spirit. We develop unconditional love by overcoming every condition presented to us that destroys our natural love, affection and regard for our spouse. When we do, we know our love is of God. "Beloved let us love one another, for love is of God: and everyone who loves is born of God and knows God."

In the pages to follow, our hope and desire is that you recognize that God gave each of us free will. We can use this freedom to choose to serve God, our "self," or another. The choice remains ours, regardless of what happens to us in marriage. We can never blame our spouse for what we choose to do with our free will. And we all must give an account to God for the choices we have made.

Our prayer is that couples discover the understanding and grace necessary to love their spouses unconditionally and by doing so abate divorce, and make marriage desirable again and preferable to cohabitation.

YOUR SPOUSE IS NOT
YOUR PROBLEM

Real Solutions for Real People

CHAPTER 1
YOUR SPOUSE IS NOT YOUR PROBLEM!
"A married couple without problems is a covenant relationship
without GOD."

OUR MARRIAGE WAS dead, or so we thought! She was
fed up with me and I with her. We both believed in God and
believed our response to God was near perfect. It was the
other that refused to change, refused to participate, refused
to cooperate. We each had given a hundred and ten percent
and we were tired. We both felt hurt, disappointment and
anger.

And we were only eight months into our first year of
marriage! Remaining married forty plus years like both sets
of our parents was incomprehensible. Weekly counseling
turned monthly and we felt we were making progress.
However, we still were uncertain about the potential
longevity of our union. We performed our roles and
responsibilities—"duties," but our hearts remained separate.
We did not know how on earth God could make the two of us
one and whether we would even like it! But God was indeed
up to something, as we would later learn.

God Is Up To Something

Marriage is not a lifeless institution! Nor does it simply
contain the lives of the male and female who enter into it.
Marriage is a vehicle, fueled by the life of God. It has a
driver—the Holy Spirit. It has a destination—the character
of Jesus Christ. God promised His Son someone like
Himself. One day may we experience the joy of being
presented to Christ. Until then, we are being prepared for
this presentation. Read Romans 8:29 - 30:

> God knew what He was doing from the very beginning. He
> decided from the outset to shape the lives of those who love Him

11

along the same lines as the life of His Son. The Son stands first in the line of humanity He restored. We see the original and intended shape of our lives there in Him. After God made that decision of what His children should be like, He followed it up by calling people by name. After He called them by name, He set them on a solid basis with Himself. And then, after getting them established, He stayed with them to the end, gloriously completing what He had begun. ("The Message")

MARRIAGE IS DESIGNED TO CHANGE US. When we receive Christ's death and resurrection as a substitute for our own, we come into right standing with God. Our spirit is recreated into His image. However, the way we think, feel and respond goes essentially unchanged. Preparation continues with the renewing of our mind and developing new responses to old and recurring problems. Marriage is designed to challenge the way we think, frustrate the way we respond and offer us opportunities to employ new ways of thinking and responding.

Marital fulfillment is the by-product of yielding to God's way of thinking and behaving. This concept, that marriage is intended to change us, is a difficult one to understand. Even more difficult is the notion that marital happiness depends on us changing. And perhaps most difficult is the idea that we even need to change.

Everybody Has Problems

Problems are an indication that change is needed. In this book, a problem is defined as any source of mystery, perplexity, great suffering, or conflict characterized by a mental struggle resulting from incompatible or opposing carnal or spiritual demands in your life. Man, male and female, will always be confronted with problems to solve. God said that it was not good for man to be alone. Therefore, in verse 18 of Genesis 2, GOD said of Adam, "I will make him a helper comparable to him." GOD makes

12

Man a helper appropriate to his needs, so that Man could be and become all that God intended.

We get married to solve the problem of aloneness. God said that it was not good for man to be alone. Imagine Adam's delight before he fell into a deep sleep. God had to devise a way to awaken his desire for an "other." You recall the rest of the story. God formed every beast of the field and brought them to Adam in pairs to see what he would name them. Now picture Adam sitting on a rock in the middle of a lush green Garden of Eden, water flowing in the distance. Picture animals presenting themselves to Adam in twos— male and female. Perhaps the first several pairs strike no chord in Adam. But with each successive pair and the naming that follows, a cutting takes place inside of Adam; a chord is struck; a desire is born. An inner awakening begins.

With Adam asleep, God slipped His hand into his side, removed a rib and shaped female. What a mystery? She was inside of Adam all along. God cut her out, gave her form and substance and then returned her to Adam. Upon being presented with his other, Adam called her, "Woman," because she was bone of his bone and flesh of his flesh. As one, they shared God's Spirit, free will, longing for one another, and something called humanness.

Your relationship with your spouse should be a mirror image of the substance necessary to join the union of Christ and the Church. Your spouse has been lovingly tasked by Christ to shine the light in dark places that hinder you from growing into a covenant relationship with Christ. Your relationship with Christ is not dependent on the behavior of your spouse.

God Is All There Is

Let's rewind a moment to when God was all there was. John 1 says that in the beginning was the Word and the Word was with God and the Word was God. God was all there was. He was all, in all and through all. And wherever God went; there He was. God had a problem! Amazing! We think so too! But being all there was, God was unable to see Himself. In order to see, scientists tell us we need an object and light to bounce off of the object to send a reflection back to us. Seems scientists only discovered what God already knew.

He created the earth—an object and then He created light. After that, He created more objects for the light to spring back reflections to Himself. But each time God solved a problem, a new challenge emerged. Of all that God created... plants, animals and minerals, none could befriend Him. None were created in His image, that is, none shared His Spirit or nature, although all came from Him. So, He created mankind in His image and after His likeness. For the first time, God had someone other than Himself with whom He could connect.

Mankind not only shared God's Spirit, but was also given one of the most loving, remarkably dangerous gifts one could bestow upon another---free will. Mankind had the freedom to choose whom he would love, whether it meant returning God's love or not. What a risk for one to take with another! What a cliffhanger! Consider loving someone so much that you offer them everything you are and everything you have. And then you give them the freedom not to choose you and be willing to accept their decision. This is what God offered and bestowed upon us!

So if God was all there was and all there is and all creation was cut out of Him, then all we say and do is in relationship to Him. Moreover, when we said, "I do" or "I will" during our marriage vows, we in fact entered into a covenant relationship with God. Now it might sound kind of funny if when asked if we are married, we replied, "I'm covenanted." First of all, many of us are still coming to grips with what this really means. Secondly, to say we are married is so much easier and invites fewer questions.

But the truth remains: marriage is a covenant—God's covenant. Marriage is perfectly flawless. It has no problems of its own. But all who enter in will attest that marriage certainly exposes the imperfections, flaws and problems within us. Likely, you are not yet convinced that these problems are yours. Besides your imperfections and flaws are comparatively minor to those of your spouse, right? That's what we think at least.

Mankind Also Had A Desire

Like God, mankind—male and female—have a desire see themselves. Albeit, Adam was content until God awoke this desire by having him see and name pairs of animals. When we were single we were all there was. Everywhere we went, there we were. We could not see ourselves. Unlike Adam, many of us searched for our "other." We prayed, presented God with lists of desired traits and thanked Him for our mates. Some of us waited. And some of us did not.

Dating compounds the problem of seeing our "self." We date each other's strengths. Our strengths are our muscles, developed in the gymnasium of adversity. Our strengths are the skills we developed and successfully used to negotiate relationships prior to marriage. They are what we learned to do, not who we are. In fact, our strengths effectively disguise who we really are and what we really need. Marriage is more concerned with who we are, rather than what we do. We date each other's strengths, but we marry

15

each other's weaknesses. When we date, we touch each other's wants. When we marry we touch each other's wounds. Dating is pleasurable. Marriage is painful—at least temporarily.

When dating, Carol was attracted to Brian's cooperative, relaxed and easygoing manner. Brian enjoyed Carol being well organized, attentive to detail and successful. Brian's strength and finesse was in his ability to relate to others. He was charming, inviting and forgiving to a fault. Carol was skillful, resourceful and an extremely high achiever. She was focused, intense and driven. Like pigeons to a homing device, so were Carol and Brian to one another.

They dated and experienced what they could be. It felt good—in fact so good they decided to marry. However, shortly after marrying, Carol was convinced Brian was unmotivated, lazy and irresponsible. Brian was certain Carol was impersonal, unaffectionate and uncaring. Together they were the epitome of form and function. Brian had all the right words and presented himself well, however, he lacked substance that comes from experience. He made a great appearance. Carol seldom had the right words—she was blunt and often arrogant. She was more concerned with the functionality of things rather than the style and appearance of them. Like so many, Brian and Carol dated each other's strengths because they complimented their own weaknesses. Neither thought marriage would dare ask them to trade.

Marriage Offers Us Solutions To The Problem Of Who We Are

To ourselves, we are not a problem. Nor do we think of ourselves as the problem. And comparatively speaking we may not be—at least when the comparisons we make are against one another.

However, Paul tells us in II Corinthians 10:12:

> For we dare not class ourselves or compare ourselves with those who commend themselves. But they, measuring themselves by themselves, and comparing themselves among themselves, are not wise.

When we compare ourselves to one another or to ourselves for that matter, we will always feel like we are better or worse than we really are. This causes many of us to be deceived about ourselves.

Danielle thought she was compassionate compared to her husband. He rarely extended grace to others and was even critical of himself. One night, Danielle was reading the account of Jesus dying on the cross. Upon reaching the part when He was being mocked, Danielle said that it was almost as if the scene were being relived before her. She became angry and felt herself wanting to intervene, but when she looked up and Jesus' eyes caught hers, He stayed her with these words, "Forgive them for they do not understand what they are doing." For the first time, Danielle was able to see just how little compassion she really had.

It is much easier to see the problems in our spouse, while we are blind to our own. Matthew encourages us to take the beam out of our own eyes that we might be able to see well enough to take the speck out of our brother's eye. Actually, whatever we are able to see in our spouse, the same lies within us. In fact, it is only that which is in us that allows us to see it in another. In Hebrews 2:11, Paul writes it this way of Jesus:

> For both He who sanctifies and those who are being sanctified *are* all one, for which reason He is not ashamed to call them brethren...

Jesus Christ is married to the Church. He is married to us. When He said, "I will" it was to His Father. Jesus entered into a covenant with His Father and we became the primary beneficiaries. Moreover, it was what Jesus accomplished with the Father that is responsible for our joy and fulfillment in relationship with Him today.

A parting thought to consider is that Jesus did not have our cooperation initially. Read Romans 5:8:

> But God demonstrates His own love toward us, in that while we were still sinners, Christ died for us.

CHAPTER 2
HEY! WAIT A MINUTE—WHAT IF I DIDN'T KNOW THAT?

"By entering into this covenant relationship, you gave GOD permission to use your spouse to encourage and provoke you to change into the image of Jesus Christ."

MOST PEOPLE DON'T know this! Let's face it, how many of us were told that marriage was going to kill us? Yet, haven't we all felt like we were dying whether by suffocation or sheer exhaustion? But the good news is that God still has the power to raise the dead!

To appreciate this small, but intense little book, you'll have to remember that God has one agenda. Hard to believe, I know. But He does! God's agenda is to change you: your soul—the way you think, feel and respond into the way He originally created you. You were created to think and behave in a manner that reflects God. You were created to live God's Life here on earth. Something went woefully wrong. So He sent Jesus Christ to live God's Life on earth. He did and He is our example. We that accept Christ have the opportunity to begin again. Marriage is one such opportunity. So you see the primary purpose of marriage is not to make you happy. It is supposed to make you different, more like Jesus.

When You Said, "I Do"

Just like so many of us were not told we would experience dying in marriage, we also were not told what we were really saying when we said, "I do" for some and "I will" for others. So let us tell you what God understood you to be saying.

When you said, "I do" or "I will" God heard this prayer:

Dear God,

I am requesting that You use (insert the name of your spouse) to be the primary one to encourage me and provoke me to change back into Your likeness. This person touches my wants, but You intend they also touch my needs (my wounds). I trust You know what I really need. Since I would not have intentionally chosen for anyone to touch the wounds that lie beneath my needs—the wounds You desperately desire to heal; You allowed me to see, experience and choose my end from the beginning. Therefore, I thank You for graciously accepting my choice of partners as Your own.

Moreover, I am requesting to be the primary one that You use to encourage and provoke my spouse to change back into Your likeness. By making this request, I am giving my life into Your hands for use on (your spouse's name) behalf.

Thank You for accepting my life as the currency, payment in full, to make the changes we (You and I) desire to see in (insert your spouse's name) life.

Now whether or not you intended to say all this is quite another thing. But this is what God understood and began acting upon when you said, "I do." You see, marriage is like a life insurance policy: one person pays the premium; another person receives the benefit. We call the recipient the primary beneficiary. Now the one that pays the premium does not receive the benefit. The benefit is dispersed upon the death of the one paying the premium. Getting married is equivalent to taking out a life insurance policy for our spouse. We agree to pay the premium and name our spouse as the primary beneficiary. And then the payments begin. It's easy at first because your spouse appears cooperative and grateful. Misunderstandings are minor and perceived as unintentional.

The deliciously tasteful experience of what we could be, still lingers. Like apples of gold in picture frames of silver, hope of marital fulfillment remains bright.

Blessed, Broken And Served

Jesus allowed God to show us how He intended to transfer seed and cultivate character. You will note each time Jesus took bread, He did three things: He blessed it, broke it and then served it. Matthew writes:

> And as they were eating, Jesus **took bread, blessed** and **broke it,** and **gave** it to the disciples and said, "Take, eat; this is My body. (Matthew 26:26)

Mark records:

> And as they were eating, Jesus **took bread, blessed** and **broke it,** and **gave** it to them and said, "Take, eat; this is My body. (Mark 14:22)

And Luke agrees:

> And He **took bread, gave thanks** and **broke** it, and **gave** it to them, saying, "This is My body which is given for you; do this in remembrance of Me. (Luke 22:19)

Paul repeats this practice in I Corinthians 11:23 - 24:

> For I received from the Lord that which I also delivered to you: that the Lord Jesus on the *same* night in which He was betrayed **took bread**; and when He had **given thanks,** He **broke** it and said, "**Take, eat**; this is My body which is broken for you; do this in remembrance of Me.

21

John, who observed and participated in this practice records one of Jesus' most thought provoking statements:

> **I am** the living **bread,** which came down from heaven. If anyone eats of this **bread,** he will live forever; and the **bread** that **I** shall give **is** My flesh, which **I** shall give for the **life** of the world.

Jesus is married to a bride. She is referred to as the Bride of Christ in Revelations 21:2 - 9:

> Then I, John, saw the holy city, New Jerusalem, coming down out of heaven from God, prepared as a bride adorned for her husband.

Cities are comprised of people. New Jerusalem is both a place and a people. It is a prepared place for a prepared people, collectively and affectionately called the bride.

> Then one of the seven angels who had the seven bowls filled with the seven last plagues came to me and talked with me, saying, 'Come, **I will show you the bride, the Lamb's wife.'**

Jesus is the lamb. Read John 1:29 - 36:

> The next day **John saw Jesus** coming toward him, **and said,** 'Behold! The Lamb of God** who takes away the sin of the world!'

> And **looking at Jesus** as he walked, **he said,** 'Behold the **Lamb of God!'**

I Got It, But What Does All This Have To Do With Me?

You, too, are married. You have a spouse, affectionately at one time called the bride or groom. Each of you brings bread or substance to the table you intended to share. For those daring to venture further, you did not simply bring bread—you are the bread! Your thoughts, attitudes, beliefs, feelings and learned responses make up your substance. Jesus called this substance bread or "life."

> Jesus said to him, '**I am the way, the truth, and the life.**' No one comes to the Father except through Me." (John 14:6)

And yet nowhere is the distinction of lives more apparent than in the "Garden of Gethsemane."

> Then He (Jesus) said to them, "My soul is exceedingly sorrowful, even to death. Stay here and watch with Me." He went a little farther and fell on His face, and prayed, saying, '**O My Father, if it is possible, let this cup pass from Me; nevertheless, not as I will, but as You** *will.*'

Here, Jesus had a mind other than His Father's. In expressing, Himself to His Father, we see the first recording of Jesus distinguishing His substance from His Father's substance: His life from His father's life. In the end and for us thankfully so, Jesus chooses His Father's life and way over His own. This is absolutely remarkable!

But even more staggering and perhaps upsetting, given your present experience in marriage, is Paul's instruction in Philippians 2:5 - 8:

> **Let this mind be in you which was also in Christ Jesus**, who, being in the form of God, did not consider it robbery to be equal with God, but made Himself of no reputation, taking the form of a bondservant, *and* coming in the likeness of man. And being found in appearance as a man, He humbled Himself and became obedient to *the point of* death, even the death of the cross.

It just doesn't seem fair! It's not! But it is justice—God's justice. It was not fair that Jesus should die for something He did not do. But He did so because God decided it righteous. It was the most loving act ever done—the innocent for the guilty. Justice fulfilled, as we read in verses 9 - 11:

Therefore, God also has highly exalted Him and given Him the name that is above every name, that at the name of Jesus every knee should bow, of those in heaven, and of those on earth, and of those under the earth, and *that* every tongue should confess that Jesus Christ *is* Lord, to the glory of God the Father.

You Were Blessed

Not only do you have life but that life, together with another life, was blessed and set apart for God on your wedding day. You received words of affirmation, prayers of consecration, and gifts from well-wishers, and so on. It was exciting! It was supposed to be. You believed the dream of being one with another.

Then some of us took off to far away places; others, to a not so far away place. Nearly all stole away to be alone—just you and your spouse! You celebrated this new life you embarked on together as Mr. and Mrs. You came as close to being one as humanly possible through sexual intercourse. You delighted in each other. As it was when dating, for the next several days—perhaps weeks (if you were lucky) you were consumed with each other. It is an "I"deal relationship. It's all about **you** and how **you** feel with your spouse. We are self-indulgent. Then reality breaks in and sends the first of many blows to "self."

You Must Be Broken

Unlike God, we try to serve our spouse unbroken bread and get mad when they spit it out. Just try stuffing a whole loaf of bread in your mouth at one time! See what happens. A popular misconception is that marriage completes us. The truth is we come complete. Albeit, we are imperfect; we are nonetheless complete. We bring a whole person to marriage. We can bring a whole loaf of bread home from the store and just as that whole loaf of bread can contain mold, rendering

24

it inedible; so we come to marriage whole, but contain impurities that make us inedible.

Jesus' first miracle was performed at a wedding. He turned water into wine. Consider what the master of the wedding feast said to the bridegroom after being presented the new wine in John 2: 9-10

> When the master of the feast had tasted the water that was made wine, and did not know where it came from [but the servants who had drawn the water knew], the master of the feast called the bridegroom. And he said to him, '**Every man at the beginning sets out the good wine, and when the *guests* have well drunk, then the inferior.**' You have kept the good wine until now!'

In the beginning of marriage, we put our best foot forward. We do our best, give our best, love our best and when we mess up, we try our best. But the recurring failure to live up to our spouse's expectations takes a toll on the best of us. We get weaker and weaker, pining away to almost nothing. We have no more to give. We're tired, hurt and angry. We're tired because we have done our best. We're hurt because our efforts didn't bring about the desired results. And we get angry because we feel unappreciated and taken advantage of by the spouse that is supposed to love us.

By now, marriage feels like an "Or"deal. Self-indulgent becomes self-protective. Our spouse's way of thinking and behaving threatens our life, that is, the way we think and behave. You've given your best and now you feel threatened, like someone's trying to take you out—on purpose! Not only is hope of marital fulfillment fading, but your total existence is endangered. We're not suggesting that you're supposed to smile and like it, nor are we unmindful that it takes two to make a relationship work! Marriage is not an amusement ride, but we do ask that you keep your hands in the vehicle at all times and refuse to take matters into your own hands. Hasn't this already proved futile?

Maybe you will find consolation in knowing that you and God make two! And God desires the same changes to take place in your spouse as you do. If He is for you, then who can be against you? So you see, not even your spouse can be your problem! Proverbs 16:7 reads:

> When a man's ways please the LORD, He makes even his enemies to be at peace with him.

So herein lies the problem: while you and God agree upon the changes that need to take place in your spouse, you disagree upon the method chosen to bring this about. God has been gracious to allow us to go first and to try it our way. And we have what we have! We served ourselves. We have nothing desirable to show for it. Read Isaiah 55:8 - 9:

> For my thoughts are not your thoughts, neither are your ways My ways," declares the LORD. For as the heavens are higher than the earth, so are My ways higher than your ways, and My thoughts than your thoughts.

And consider Proverbs 14:12:

> There is a way that seems right to a man, but its end is the way of death.

And if this isn't enough, consider some of Jeremiah's words to God's people in Jeremiah 4:18:

> Your ways and your doings have brought these things upon you...

Unfortunately, most discontented spouses never even get to consider these things. They get fed up and are convinced their spouse is the problem. At least one out of every two husbands or wives decides they deserve better, calls it quits

26

and files for divorce. This includes Christians. It seems that our faith fails us at a time when we need it the most.

You Must Be Served

Since when did God begin advocating serving ourselves? Oh, I know you, like so many others, bought into the misconception that God helps those who help themselves. Perhaps these are well-meaning words to encourage personal responsibility, but they are poisonous to our spiritual well being.

Jesus declared Himself the bread of life. He revealed the method God would use to change people. And then God demonstrated this method using His own Son. Now if God would not spare His only begotten Son, do we really believe that He would spare us?

We cannot serve our "self" and God. We cannot do it our way and God's way at the same time. Our ways oppose one another. We have to choose. Read Matthew 6:24:

> No one can serve two masters; for either he will hate the one and love the other, or else he will be loyal to the one and despise the other. You cannot serve God and mammon.

We typically read this scripture as it relates to money. Money represents substance. For some, substance might mean intellect and we all know people that have gone to the bank on their intellect! For others, substance might mean their physical appearance and we all know people that have gone to the bank on their looks! Less apparent, though, is the substance comprised of what we think and how we think and relate to others.

God's plan is to serve us to our spouse. That is, God desires to serve your character, strengths, skills and abilities to your spouse. But He cannot and, therefore, will not serve

27

what has not been blessed and broken. Once broken, God can teach us new ways of thinking and responding that will infuse life into our spouse and also revive us.

We need to be revived to participate in God's life. Remember, God's primary agenda is to remake us into the image and likeness of His Son. I take comfort in these words in Philippians 1:6:

> ...being confident of this very thing, that He who has begun a good work in you will complete *it* until the day of Jesus Christ.

CHAPTER 3
WHY ME?

Therefore, you must live in such a way that your spouse and all those God has given you to influence have every opportunity to enter into a covenant relationship with GOD."

WHY NOT YOU? You made a covenant with God; your spouse is the primary beneficiary. As you are remade into God's image, you free up your assets, that is, your way of thinking and behaving for use by another. By liquidating your assets, they become available for immediate use. God has been waiting a long time to have access and to gain the use of our assets—which is to say, our life.

Our spouse needs our life. And when God has our life in His hand, He is able to meet our spouse's need. Just because we know what our spouse needs does not mean we are qualified to give it to him or her. In fact, the motivations behind our most charitable acts of kindness are often impure and self-serving. It is only when our spouses come into contact with God that permanent and lasting change is possible. And you do want your spouse to change, don't you? So let's consider further the idea of currency and the motivations behind our spending.

What many are just beginning to realize is that God set up the whole idea of currency, not man. There are over 2000 scriptures in the Bible as it relates to money. Currency is the medium used to exchange one thing for another. Every kingdom has its own currency. Most kingdoms have the equivalent of a Treasury Department, which manages the currency system with the intent of promoting the conditions for prosperity and stability of their respective kingdoms.

The world's currency system is money. Given the country, money may be known by different names and forms. Nonetheless, all use it to deal and trade in the world. We learn the power of money when we use it to get what we desire. We give the retailer cash; we get the item we purchased. Now what we give and get back are not the same. We give cash; we get clothes. Before the exchange, however, we agree that the value of the cash and the value of the clothing is the same. I Corinthians 15 tells us that what is given to the earth does not come up in the appearance that it was given. We sow a seed; it comes up a plant. A seed dies; a plant emerges. Moreover, John 12:24 tells us:

> Most assuredly, I say to you, unless a grain of wheat falls into the ground and dies, it remains alone; but if it dies, it produces much grain.

When we give our money to purchase something, our money is gone, but the value of what we purchased is desired more than the money we gave for it. That money doesn't return to us. But if we are happy with our purchase, we are not sad in having parted with our money. Buyer's remorse does occur, usually when we feel such regret in believing we paid too much, or we realize we really cannot afford what we purchased. And then, sometimes, we discover what we purchased is not what we wanted after all.

We can use money anywhere in the world. It works. It does what it is designed to do. It serves its purpose faithfully. Even in the cases in which we have to convert our money into the format of that in another kingdom, it still works. In the world, to buy and sell, we need money. The more we have the better off we are. The kicker, get this, is even if we don't take part in the system of currency in a given kingdom it is not rendered disabled—we simply cannot exchange goods. This is not a matter of a kingdoms likes or dislikes for a person, but a matter of economy.

The Currency Of The Kingdom

The currency of God's Kingdom is the sacrifice (of life).

God established the economy of His Kingdom from the foundation of the world as it is written in Revelation 13:8:

> And all the inhabitants of the earth will fall down in adoration and pay Him homage, everyone whose name has not been recorded in the Book of Life of the Lamb that was slain [in sacrifice] from the foundation of the world. (Amplified Version)

And we read what happened when Adam and Eve disobeyed God and sewed fig leaves together to cover their sin in Genesis 3:7:

> Then the eyes of both of them were opened, and they knew that they *were* naked; and they sewed fig leaves together and made themselves coverings.

God condemned their actions. He then revealed His method for redeeming or buying man back. Read Genesis 3:21:

> Also for Adam and his wife the LORD God made tunics of skin, and clothed them.

Adam, Eve and God agreed on their need for covering. They disagreed, however, on the method chosen to accomplish this. Adam and Eve chose a leaf from a tree that kept its life. God chose an animal to give up its life so that Adam and Eve might regain life. You and God agree on many of the changes that need to occur in your spouse. At least up until now, you simply disagreed on the method used to bring these changes about. Therefore, you misunderstood the opportunities to participate with God and declined by default.

Read what Paul says about the currency of God's Kingdom in Hebrews 9:12 - 14:

> He also bypassed the sacrifices consisting of goat and calf blood, instead using His own blood as the price to set us free once and for all. If that animal blood and the other rituals of purification were effective in cleaning up certain matters of our religion and

behavior, think how much more the blood of Christ cleans up our whole lives, inside and out.

Isaiah 53:10 reads:

> Still, it's what GOD had in mind all along, to crush him with pain. The plan was that He give Himself as an offering for sin so that He'd see life come from it--life, life, and more life. ("The Message")

But That Was Jesus and He Paid It All

You may be thinking, "But, I am not Jesus!" No you are not and no one expects you to be. "But didn't He die once and for all?" Yes, the work is finished. Our lives as believers should provide evidence of what has already been accomplished. This occurs when we allow Christ to live fully and completely in us.

In Galatians 2:20, we learn the mindset we are to adopt as Christians:

> I have been crucified with Christ [in Him I have shared His crucifixion]; it is no longer I who live, but Christ [the Messiah] lives in me; and the life I now live in the body I live by faith in [by adherence to and reliance on and complete trust in] the Son of God, Who loved me and gave Himself up for me.

Let's rewind for a moment and reconsider God's primary agenda. God is remaking us into His image and likeness. How does He do this? By blessing us, breaking us and serving us. And this is not a "one time only" and it's over occurrence. Just as the natural body has a penchant for food, so does your spiritual body.

Consider how many meals you eat in a day, a week, a month or even a year. In anticipation of a majority of them you sat down with the food in front of you, you bowed your head and blessed the food and the hands that prepared it. Then you might have asked God to make it nourishing, or beneficial to the sustaining of your body. Then many of those times you picked up your knife and fork, cut your food into edible portions and began to eat. We perform this ritual everyday of our lives, except when given to fasting. Now if things we can see can help us understand and grasp spiritual truths, here is one we ought to grasp. God blesses whom He intends to break. And He only breaks what He intends to serve.

In marriage, we will be blessed, broken and served many times. In our house, leftovers are good for about a day, if that. We cannot live off of leftovers, no more than we can live off of past testimonies concerning that which God has brought us through. Testimonies get old. The decay of an unchanging life grows upon them, like mold grows on bread. They become inedible over time. And just as we would not serve our families bread with mold on it, God will not serve us to our spouse with mold on us.

The decay must be destroyed and removed.

> We know that our old [unrenewed] self was nailed to the cross with Him in order that [our] body [which is the instrument] of sin might be made ineffective and inactive for evil, that we might no longer be the slaves of sin. (Romans 6:6—Amplified Version)

Since Christ incurred the judgment and paid the penalty for our sin, many Christians believe there should be no amount of pain or suffering expected by a Christian. But the Bible vigorously refutes this view. Just take a look at these scriptures:

> Yes, and all who desire to live godly in Christ Jesus will suffer persecution. (II Timothy 3:12)

> Therefore let those who suffer according to the will of God commit their souls to Him in doing good, as to a faithful Creator. (I Peter 4:19)

> Since Jesus went through everything you're going through and more, learn to think like Him. Think of your sufferings as a weaning from that old sinful habit of always expecting to get your own way. (I Peter 4:1, "The Message")

> I now rejoice in my sufferings for you, and fill up in my flesh what is lacking in the afflictions of Christ, for the sake of His body, which is the church. (Colossians 1:24)

Timothy, Peter and Paul confirm that there is a suffering that we will experience as Christians. Timothy says **we will suffer** and Peter adds that it is God's will that we suffer. Earlier Peter said that when we suffer, we cease from wanting, even demanding our own way. Love does not insist on having its own way (I Corinthians 13:5). And then Paul tells us that we will suffer so that others can experience God.

God's Word Cuts Deeply

Cutting destroys the body of decay, while transforming and releasing the life inside. Now consider that the word states "the life... is in the blood" (Leviticus 17:11). People die when the heart ceases to discharge blood throughout the body. Blood without oxygen is dark red and appears blue through some skins. This is the blood in the veins. Blood with oxygen is bright red; it is found in the arteries. It's the same blood, in different forms. The arteries carry oxygen-rich blood to the organs. The veins transport oxygen-depleted blood back to the heart. Life is released from the heart, carried by available vessels called arteries, and received by the organs that need it. The organs, in return, release waste products into the blood into other vessels called veins whose job it is to take the life deprived blood back to the heart.

34

This is a wonderful illustration of what takes place in marriage. The Bible says that the two shall become one. Together, husband and wife represent one body. God is the heart of this body, we are arteries and our spouse is the veins. This means that God intends to transport our oxygen–rich life to our spouse and for our spouse to deplete our life by secreting wastes that necessitate a return to the heart. Paul said it this way of Jesus in Hebrews 2:11:

> For both He Who sanctifies [making men holy] and those who are sanctified all have one [Father]. For this reason He is not ashamed to call them brethren... (Amplified Version)

We all have one Source—one common origin and destination. The natural body's source is the heart. The marital body's Source is God. All life that is meaningful and fulfilling must circulate through the Source. In order for God to bring about the changes you desire to see in your spouse, He will need your cooperation. You will need to develop intentional responses to God so that those He has given you to influence have every opportunity to enter into a deeper relationship with Him. God will mix your lives together allowing the character strengths in you to cleanse and bring healing to the character weaknesses in your spouse and vice versa.

We understand and even enjoy the exchanging of lives during sexual intercourse. However, when it comes to exchanging our life when we have not understood why and pain is our nightly bedfellow, we naturally resist. We just believe there is something wrong here.

Marriage is a life for a life. It's not a 50-50 arrangement as some suppose. It costs us everything—literally. Both our fulfillment and our spouse's transformation are a by-product of developing God-directed, intentional responses in relationship to our partner. We must get this!

The Goods We Can Purchase In The Kingdom

The goods of the Kingdom are character related. Some of the goods available for purchase in the kingdom are: honesty, diligence, virtue, knowledge, self-control, perseverance, godliness, kindness and meekness, to name a few. If you are routinely irritated and compromised by your spouse's lack of character, you have what they need. Your challenge will be in learning how to offer it in such a way that he or she might receive it. But by giving your life for your spouse, you gain personal and marital fulfillment.

CHAPTER 4
GOT MARITAL FULFILLMENT?

"My frustrations, irritations and at times lack of marital fulfillment
prove that my best efforts have failed and will continue to fail to
produce the marriage GOD intends for me."

START HERE. Discard some basic myths about marriage, three of which guarantee marital unhappiness. They are: 1) Meeting each other's perceived needs results in marital fulfillment; 2) Negotiating and compromising with each other will result in marital fulfillment; and 3) Poor communication is the biggest problem between husbands and wives. Let's take a closer look at these myths.

Meeting Each Other's Needs

The first myth is meeting each other's perceived needs results in marital fulfillment. Much has been written about our needs as men and women and husbands and wives. We all, at one time or another, have earnestly tried to meet our spouses needs as they perceived them, as the experts have defined them, and as we understood them. Now let me ask you a question, "Since having intentionally tried to answer your spouse's needs, are you really any happier? Is your spouse? Oftentimes, what we define as our needs, are better called "wants." When needs are answered, satisfaction is the result. When wants are answered, we typically lust for more. Greed is the result. Needs are answered and we experience fulfillment; wants are ongoing and therefore, we experience a lack of fulfillment.

Needs have to do with those things that are necessary to promote and maintain life. Wants are those things that are not required to sustain life, but make life more comfortable. We all have natural needs and spiritual needs. Food is a natural need, while conformity to Christ is a spiritual need. If we do not digest bread and water, we will die physically.

If we do not digest Christ, we will die spiritually. Those that do not have Christ are dead already.

It's just that simple. We may want Starbucks coffee, but we don't need it to live. Similarly, we may want miracles, but we do not need them to live spiritually. God determined what things would be needed to sustain both our natural lives and our spiritual lives. Confusing needs with wants inevitably leads to marital discontentment.

Negotiating And Compromise

Solving problems by giving a little and taking a little is the second myth that also unavoidably ends in marital unhappiness. While this widely used method of resolving conflict deludes us with temporary improvements, it rarely ever gets to the heart of the matter in conflict. Marriage is intended to break us down. To do so in the presence of one another is dreadfully painful to our ego.

Marital happiness is not a realistic goal. It is not something to be pursued. It is a by-product of our conformity to Christ. And this we ought to pursue. Negotiation and compromise only delay our need to conform to Christ. Bargaining, reaching a deal and reducing it to writing are fine ways to handle business transactions; however, marriage is not a contractual arrangement involving objects.

Marriage is a covenant for the purpose of changing and reproducing lives. From God's perspective, the only paper involved is the marriage license that is the pre-approval necessary to undergo the process of change! Those that insist on taking a business approach to marriage will be disappointed in the long run.

Communication vs. Connection

Couples and experts alike agree with this third myth: that poor communication is likely the biggest problem between husbands and wives. Reliable, self-reporting couples, psychologists and therapists say this. The bookshelves at local retailers are loaded with books on communicating more effectively. But, we beg to differ. In order to argue, a few things are clear. One, husbands and wives understand what each is saying. Two, both disagree with what the other is saying. And three, each values his or her own opinion over the other. Since the opinions expressed represent different and competing realities, each makes a choice to hold on to what is personally believed. A message has been sent. An unacceptable response was returned. The couple has effectively communicated. But they have not connected. In fact, they now have relative distance between them. The relative distance can be measured by the personal significance of the issue over which they disagree. If the issue has enormous significance and huge implications for one or both, then the distance between them is probably massive.

The greatest challenge couples experience is connecting and reconnecting after a breakdown. When the breakdowns are recurring, the desire and will of the participants to work through the difficulties declines. Couples tend to slip willfully and yet unknowingly into a comatose state. Exhausted by opposition from without and spent within by futile efforts to respond in the only way each knows how are ingredients for divorce. It is a critical juncture in marriage.

Imagine being so excited to go on vacation—you absolutely couldn't wait! Since it was about sun and fun, little clothing was needed. You placed a backpack on your shoulder, darted out of the house and began walking to the airport hoping to catch a ride. After walking vigorously for a couple of hours, you tire, begin to sweat, feel hunger set in and the need for relief. You stop and bend over to catch your breath only to discover you have been on a treadmill the entire time! Did you expend energy with the intention of reaching your vacation spot of rest and relaxation? Are you any closer to your destination? How might you feel? Angry? Hurt? Depressed? Nearly all of us experience this at one time or another in marriage.

Honestly, at this point are we really interested in connecting or relief? If you are like most, it is here that sinful diversions and other distractions seem most appealing. What are we looking for at this point? Connection, connection, connection! We communicated, but we failed to connect with our target. We exerted effort. We're tired and in pain. Now we just want it fixed—and at no additional cost to ourselves. Isn't that right?

So do we retreat further and sin? Or do we, rest, evaluate, plan and adjust to accomplish our goal—marital fulfillment? Before you decide, consider Paul's words in I Corinthians 10:12 -14:

> Don't be so naive and self-confident. You're not exempt. You could fall flat on your face as easily as anyone else. Forget about self-confidence; it's useless. Cultivate God-confidence. No test or temptation that comes your way is beyond the course of what others have had to face. All you need to remember is that God will never let you down; He'll never let you be pushed past your limit; He'll always be there to help you come through it. So, my very dear friends, when you see people reducing God to something they can use or control, get out of their company as fast as you can. ("The Message")

Understandably, these are hard words for those that are weary, in pain and in the throes of death. And who hasn't felt like marriage is killing him or her at times? Marriage unrelentingly goes after our desire to live the way we want.

40

We are likely to feel suffocated or pounded to death. However, we can take comfort in knowing that God both wills and desires that we experience fulfillment and that conforming to His way of thinking and behaving is the only way to bring this about. So He had David write of His ways in Psalm 18:30:

> As for God, His way is perfect; the word of the LORD is proven; He is a shield to all who trust in Him.

And Psalm 18:32:

> It is God who arms me with strength and makes my way perfect.

God intends to connect with us, not merely communicate. Adam and Eve never lost the ability to communicate with God. They talked with one another after they sinned. However, despite communicating they were not connected. When our goal is simply to communicate better with our spouse, then our quarrels should prove that we already do this very well. But if we desire to connect, then these same quarrels prove we don't do this well. Read Psalm 18:30 again in the Message Translation:

> What a God! His road stretches straight and smooth. Every GOD-direction is road-tested. Everyone who runs toward Him makes it.

This is not merely a desire to communicate, but rather to connect. God desires to connect with us and for us to connect with our spouse. We were created to connect. We were made to connect. So, understandably this is quite a compelling desire for all.

But The Desire To Live And Be Happy Is Equally Compelling

The desire to live and be happy is so strong that it can torture us into submission. It can be belligerent. This

41

desire often pressures us to implement God's will our way and in our own strength. When things don't work out, we become frustrated, irritated, tired and disappointed. Some quit. Some do not. We pray you do not.

Consider how the silversmith refines silver. He holds a piece of silver over the fire and lets it heat up. The silver needs to be held in the middle of the fire where the flames are the hottest in order to burn away all the impurities. In past times the silversmith sat in front of the fire the entire time the silver was being refined. He had to keep his eyes on the silver the whole time the silver was in the fire. This was because if the silver remained in the flames even a moment too long, it would be destroyed. Identifying the sliver of space between the impurity of unrefined silver and the destruction of overly refined silver is the silversmith's goal. The goal is accomplished when the silversmith can see his own image in the silver.

Now remember that God's primary agenda is that we be transformed to His image. We see this in Romans 12:2. And how will He know when this is achieved? When God can see His reflection in us. And how will we know? When He appears, we will be like Him.

> Beloved, now we are children of God; and it has not yet been revealed what we shall be, but we know that when He is revealed, we shall be like Him, for we shall see Him as He is. (I John 3:2)

Now we can appreciate Malachi 3:2 - 4:

> But who can endure the day of His coming? And who can stand when He appears? For He *is* like a refiner's fire and like launderers' soap. He will sit as a refiner and a purifier of silver; He will purify the sons of Levi, and purge them as gold and silver, that they may offer to the LORD, an offering in righteousness. Then the offering of Judah and Jerusalem will be pleasant to the LORD...

Before God will deliver our strengths and gifts to our spouse, He will cleanse us first. Frustration, irritation and impatience are good indicators that there is yet cleansing that still needs to occur. Our motives must be purified. When the trace impurities of self-enlargement, self-protection and self-preservation are removed, our gifts have a more pleasing aroma. And your spouse knows the difference, oftentimes even when you do not! Read Malachi 3:2 - 4 in "The Message":

> But who will be able to stand up to that coming? Who can survive His appearance? He'll be like white-hot fire from the smelter's furnace. He'll be like the strongest lye soap at the laundry. He'll take His place as a refiner of silver, as a cleanser of dirty clothes. He'll scrub the Levite priests clean, refine them like gold and silver, until they're fit for GOD, fit to present offerings of righteousness. Then, and only then, will Judah and Jerusalem be fit and pleasing to GOD, as they used to be in the years long ago.

Let go of the idea that marital happiness is something that occurs between you and your spouse, or lies within your spouse's control. It doesn't! Past negative experiences with your spouse does not prevent you from experiencing marital fulfillment. We must get over the idea that our spouse defines our experience. God does. Husbands and wives provide each other information that either can be filtered through God or our own archives. When we filter information through God and His Word, we become spiritually minded and experience life and peace. Read Romans 8:6:

> Now the mind of the flesh [which is sense and reason without the Holy Spirit] is death [death that comprises all the miseries arising from sin, both here and hereafter]. But the mind of the [Holy] Spirit is life and [soul] peace [both now and forever]. (Amplified)

No matter how bad it might get in marriage, peace is present and available to us. We receive peace when we filter our experiences through God's Word. Unfortunately, many today, filter their spouse's behavior as well as God's word through their own experiences. Consequently, they forfeit the joy and peace God intended for them.

The Honeymoon Is Over

We have debunked a few myths; perhaps you have accepted the fact that the honeymoon's over and you still love your spouse, but you just don't like him or her! Or maybe, you love your spouse, but you are not in love with him or her. These are good indications that you have moved beyond illusions about marriage.

Unfortunately, you have held onto some delusions—not about your spouse, but about yourself! Our 9 year old daughter, Jordan in response to what God thinks about us said, "You're not nearly as good as you think you are and you're not nearly as good as you will be." The bad news is we believe some things about our "self" that simply are not true. The good news is that you are right where God wants you to be! We assure you!

When we were younger, I enjoyed the roller coasters. But it was the first hill and drop that always got me. It was usually the highest and deepest and felt like a free fall despite being on a track. My heart went from my chest to my lap in 0.3 seconds! It was scary and thrilling all at the same time. I was scared because I was completely out of control, but thrilled with excitement because the car was secured to the track. Perhaps you are still apprehensive about what you are reading. It does not fit into the institution of marriage that the world has created—an institution that you have come to strongly believe in. But rest assured, we are securely on track—God's track. He has always presided over what happens to men and women in marriage. And He knows what He is doing! Now may He give you eyes to see what He is doing.

Stop for a moment. Breathe. We have said some jaw-dropping things here. Now would be a good time to pray and ask God to help you to receive all that He intends for you from what you have read so far.

CHAPTER 5
LOST OPPORTUNITIES

"Everything your spouse does to you (good and bad) is your opportunity
to respond to GOD for the purpose of establishing Christ in you."

EVERYTHING? ABSOLUTELY EVERYTHING! God is all and in all. Everything comes from the Father, goes through the Father and returns to the Father. Although what happens to us might not be good to us, it will ultimately be good for us. God has pre-determined that some of our greatest challenges should yield the greatest benefits. He set it up this way! Jeremiah 18:4 says this as the potter was working at his wheel:

> And the vessel he was making of clay was spoiled in the potter's hand, and he reworked it into another vessel, as it seemed good to the potter to do.

We learned earlier that God desires to connect with us, not simply communicate. It is easy to confuse the two words especially when relationship is assumed. That is, it is easy to assume we are connected with God because we have received His Son and we are on speaking terms. We can talk to God and be moved by God and still not be connected.

In its most basic sense, communication means to send and receive messages. And though communication comes from the word "commune" which means to experience a deep abiding connection, believers and couples alike would agree that such intimacy with God and their spouse often eludes them. This is why we suggest that we can talk with God and He with us, and still not connect. But whenever we connect with God, communication has occurred. The same is true for husbands and wives. Substituting the two words is deceptive. Many books have been written to help couples communicate better, while these same readers starve for more intimate connection. But when questioned further many of these same couples identify intimacy as their greatest desire in marriage.

We counseled Tom and Jackie for approximately three months. Both identified their primary problem as communication. They were cordial to one another generally. But each felt unheard and unsupported in the things that really mattered to each. Financial security was important to Jackie. Tom said that Jackie was controlling and insisted on the bills being handled her way. When he delayed, she became verbally abusive and disrespectful. He responded by saying nothing and walking off.

Sex mattered to Tom. Jackie told us that their fights had become more frequent and intense just prior to meeting with us. Tom's word was bankrupt with her because he did not follow through on things they had agreed upon. She indicated having to regularly pay late fees—money they could be saving. Yet, in the bedroom he rudely demanded his sexual desires be fulfilled. When she does not comply, Jackie stated that Tom becomes angry and has punched a hole in the wall on more than one occasion. It was quickly apparent to us that Tom and Jackie understood one another very well. They simply rejected what the other was saying.

Tom resented Jackie trying to control him. Jackie took exception to Tom's sexual demands. Jackie wanted security. Tom wanted sex. They clearly understood each other. Tom and Jackie communicated. Neither accepted the message sent. They argued. Both were offended. Each disconnected from God and each other. Communication does not necessarily result in connection.

God Communicates With Everyone

God talks with saints, sinners and yes, even Satan. Throughout the gospels, we observe Jesus interacting with the disciples. He even communicated with Judas, the one who would ultimately betray Him.

After being told that eating of the tree of the knowledge of good and evil would result in death or disconnection from God, Adam and Eve ate. In Genesis Chapter three we see God communicating with Adam and Eve, the creation from which He was now disconnected. Although they remained on speaking terms, they were not connected.

And consider God's conversation with Satan. Beginning in Job 1:6, we read:

> Now there was a day when the sons of God came to present themselves before the Lord, and Satan also came among them. The Lord said to Satan, 'Whence have you come?' Satan answered the Lord, 'From going to and fro on the earth, and from walking up and down on it.' (Revised Standard Version)

It is clear that God communicates with those with whom He is not connected. Oftentimes, we find husbands and wives on speaking terms, but obviously disconnected.

God Connects With Hearts, Not Heads

While in college, a friend and I (Kim) debated whether the heart or mind was more significant in determining who a person is. Although not a Christian at the time, I was fully persuaded that the condition of one's heart mattered more than his state of mind. There was something about the heart that intrigued me.

After I became a Christian, I would catch myself thinking. And then I began to realize that there was often a thought behind my thought, or the reason why I thought a certain way was noticeable. Once I discovered this, I stopped waiting to notice my second thought and asked myself why I said or did whatever it was at the time. All this to say, I

49

discovered there were two thoughts occurring almost simultaneously—my mind's thought and my motive or heart's thought. Sometime thereafter, we decided that the motivations formed in our heart were eternally more important than the wardrobe of thoughts our mind enjoyed clothing them in.

God only connects with the heart that has received His Son, Jesus Christ. He connects with such a heart to aid in our conformity to Christ. Read John 1:12 - 13:

> But as many as received Him, to them He gave the right to become children of God, to those who believe in His name: who were born, not of blood, nor of the will of the flesh, nor of the will of man, but of God.

God connects with hearts that believe to provide authority and power for the soul to become something it is presently not. We read in Romans 10:9:

> But what does it say? *'The word is near you, in your mouth and in your heart'* [that is, the word of faith which we preach]: that if you confess with your mouth the Lord Jesus and believe in your heart that God has raised Him from the dead, you will be saved. For with the heart one believes unto righteousness, and with the mouth confession is made unto salvation.

II Corinthians tells us that whosoever is born of God is a new creation, old things have passed away, all things have become new. When we received Christ, we became what the Bible calls born again. Our spirit was recreated into the image of God—our original image before mankind's fall into sin. However, our soul was left essentially unchanged. This is why Paul writes in Romans 12:2:

> And do not be conformed to this world, but be transformed by the renewing of your mind, that you may prove what *is* that good and acceptable and perfect will of God.

Paul goes on to tell us that we ought to express outwardly the salvation of our soul in Philippians 2:12 - 13:

> Therefore, my beloved, as you have always obeyed, not as in my presence only, but now much more in my absence, work out your own salvation with fear and trembling; for it is God who works in you both to will and to do for *His* good pleasure.

In other words, it is God working inside of our hearts to bring about our conformity to Christ in both word and deed. Remember, before we were married and now after we were married, God has had one agenda all along: to remake us— spirit, soul and body into His image. He has already remade our spirit. He is now remaking our soul. And when He comes again He will complete the remaking of our bodies.

> But someone will say, 'How are the dead raised up? And with what body do they come?' Foolish one, what you sow is not made alive unless it dies. And what you sow, you do not sow that body that shall be, but mere grain—perhaps wheat or some other *grain*. But God gives it a body as He pleases, and to each seed its own body.
>
> All flesh *is* not the same flesh, but *there is* one *kind of* flesh of men, another flesh of animals, another of fish, *and* another of birds. *There are* also celestial bodies and terrestrial bodies; but the glory of the celestial *is* one, and the *glory* of the terrestrial *is* another. *There is* one glory of the sun, another glory of the moon, and another glory of the stars; for *one* star differs from *another* star in glory. So also *is* the resurrection of the dead. *The body* is sown in corruption, it is raised in incorruption. It is sown in dishonor, it is raised in glory. It is sown in weakness, it is raised in power. It is sown a natural body, it is raised a spiritual body. There is a natural body, and there is a spiritual body. And so it is written, *'The first man Adam became a living being.'* The last Adam *became* a life-giving spirit. However, the spiritual is not first, but the natural, and afterward the spiritual. The first man *was* of the earth, *made* of dust; the second Man *is* the Lord from heaven. As *was* the *man* of dust, so also *are* those *who are made* of dust; and as *is* the heavenly *Man,* so also *are* those *who are* heavenly. And as we have borne the image of the *man* of dust, we shall also bear the image of the heavenly *Man.*

51

Stop for just a minute. Now consider your thoughts the very first time you eyed the title of this book: "Your Spouse Is Not Your Problem!" What were they? Objection? Disbelief? Curiosity as to where it was leading? Whatever your initial thoughts, your second thought was to pick it up, read the back cover and skim through the table of contents and possibly read a few lines in a chapter. And now whether it was purchased or given to you, you find yourself here on this page. Hopefully, you began at the beginning. It is very likely that some of your beliefs and ideas about marriage have been challenged.

For instance, you have believed that negotiation and compromise was the best way to settle marital conflict. But now you understand and accept the futility of these methods as they leave the character Jesus came to transform in tact. By changing your mind, you are available to discover new ways to solve old, repetitive and nagging problems.

Our way of thinking and behaving must be interrupted, sometimes, severely so in order for us even to consider another way—God's way! Our spouse does a wonderfully skillful job in knowing just which one of our buttons to push. It seems pre-meditated. It feels like cruel and unusual punishment. If our spouses didn't know how they were impacting us, that would be one thing. But they know and so we assume they are in control of their behavior. Their repeated apologies and promises to change are proof that they know what they are doing and are choosing to do it on purpose. However, Romans 7:15 - 21 gives us insight into what's going on when our spouse keeps offending us:

> I can anticipate the response that is coming: 'I know that all God's commands are spiritual, but I'm not. Isn't this also your experience?' Yes. I'm full of myself—after all, I've spent a long time

in sin's prison. What I don't understand about myself is that I decide one way, but then I act another, doing things I absolutely despise. So if I can't be trusted to figure out what is best for myself and then do it, it becomes obvious that God's command is necessary.

But I need something more! For if I know the law but still can't keep it, and if the power of sin within me keeps sabotaging my best intentions, I obviously need help! I realize that I don't have what it takes. I can will it, but I can't do it. I decide to do good, but I don't really do it; I decide not to do bad, but then I do it anyway. My decisions, such as they are, don't result in actions. Something has gone wrong deep within me and gets the better of me every time. It happens so regularly that it's predictable. The moment I decide to do good, sin is there to trip me up.

Paul tells us the bottom line is that when we continue doing things we have no desire to do and are unable to do the things we desire, then it is no longer we that are in control, but rather sin within us. In order for God to remake a soul, admission must be made that its thoughts and behaviors are not under the person's control. It's like the drug addict that believes he can stop anytime, or the alcoholic that insists they don't have to drink, or the liar that can't stop lying, or the cheater that can't stop cheating.

Dana promised Don she would not cheat on him again. This was the fourth time she was discovered with another man— twice during their lengthy engagement, once in the first six months of marriage and now once again in the middle of year two. Don was beside himself. He was hurt, angry and distraught. He loved Dana and wanted to believe that she would not betray him again. Her willingness to participate in counseling was enough for Don. But we knew all too well that until Dana stopped referring to her problem as an issue that she was working on, counseling would be ineffective. Dana needed to recognize that adultery is not simply a problem, but sin. Sin was in control, not Dana.

We would love to tell you that Dana changed her mind and accepted her behavior as sinful. But during the two meetings we had with Don and Dana, she remained convinced that she could stop on her own. She felt that Don's lack of sexual availability was responsible for her behavior.

Toward the end of the second meeting Dana told us that she resented being made to feel like the culprit for their marital difficulties. Dana believed that if Don were more available to her, then there would be no need or desire for other men. Sadly enough, she stopped coming after the second session, convinced Don was the problem.

God Connects With Our Heart Through Experiences

Each day, we have countless interactions with others and many of these occur with our spouse. We call these experiences. If we are watchful and mindful of God, each experience provides us with information about our "self." We routinely overlook this important information because we generally feel good about "self," our efforts in relation to our spouse and our responsiveness to God. Proverbs 16:2 reads:

> All the ways of a man are pure in his own eyes, but the Lord weighs the spirits [the thoughts and intents of the heart]. (Amplified Version)

And since we come to interactions thinking nothing is wrong with us, whenever a problem arises it is understandable that we believe our spouse is at fault. How quickly we forget God's primary agenda with us—which is to remake us, not our spouses, into His image. Our thoughts will have to change. Our attitudes and beliefs will have to change. Our behavior will have to change. We will have to change!

54

And as Jesus said to Peter who complained about the onus being on him:

> If I will that he remain till I come, what *is that* to you? You follow Me.

Like Peter, we often think it unfair that we must do all the changing. But we gave our lives to God through Christ. Who did? We did! Hopefully, you are beginning to discover that marriage has less to do with your spouse and much more to do with who you are and who you are becoming in relationship to your spouse. Marriage is one of the primary gymnasiums God uses to develop unconditional love in us. Our failure to believe this does not alter this truth. We are being equipped and outfitted to live eternally with God. There will be no marriage among men and women in heaven. Marriage is for here and now. It is designed to produce godly character and godly offspring. Marriage also offers us a wonderful foretaste of the pleasure that awaits us in heaven.

> For in the resurrection they neither marry nor are given in marriage, but are like angels of God in heaven. (Matthew 22:30)

This may surprise some, but marriage was never intended to make us happy, but rather holy. During every interaction we have, we make a deposit and a withdrawal. God desires that we not only become aware of our contribution, but also be willing to modify our contribution at His request. God is less concerned about what we are given, but how we respond to what we have been given. In other words, God is more concerned about our response to what happens to us than what actually happens to us. Jesus said it this way in Mark 7:18 - 23:

> So He said to them, 'Are you thus without understanding also? Do you not perceive that whatever enters a man from outside cannot defile him, because it does not enter his heart but his stomach, and is eliminated, *thus* purifying all foods?' And He

said, 'What comes out of a man, that defiles a man. For from within, out of the heart of men, proceed evil thoughts, adulteries, fornications, murders, thefts, covetousness, wickedness, deceit, lewdness, an evil eye, blasphemy, pride, foolishness; All these evil things come from within and defile a man.'

The emphasis here is on what proceeds from us. Stated even more plainly, we read Jesus' words in Luke 6:45:

A good man out of the good treasure of his heart brings forth good; and an evil man out of the evil treasure of his heart brings forth evil. For out of the abundance of the heart his mouth speaks.

Interactions have a way of revealing to us that care to know, what is in us. We need help in seeing our heart because:

The heart is deceitful above all things, and it is exceedingly perverse and corrupt and severely, mortally sick! Who can know it [perceive, understand, be acquainted with his own heart and mind]? (Jeremiah 17:9, Amplified Version)

Only God, He that knows everything about everything there is anything to know about, truly knows the complexity of our hearts—our true thoughts and motivations. And He is more than willing to share what He knows about us with us who desire to know. To test our willingness to know how we really are, God offers us tons of opportunities in a given day. They are called interactions or experiences.

Oh, let the wickedness of the wicked come to an end, but establish the just; For the righteous God tests the hearts and minds. (Psalm 7:9)

The refining pot is for silver and the furnace for gold, But the LORD **tests** the **hearts**. (Proverbs 17:3)

I said in my heart, 'Concerning the condition of the sons of men, God tests them, that they may see that they themselves are like animals.' (Ecclesiastes 3:18)

> Examine me, O LORD, and prove me; Try my mind and my heart. (Psalm 26:2)

God gives us generous opportunities because He realizes that conformity to Christ requires that we make choices between who we are and who He would have us to be. Without information we would be unable to make a choice. So He both sends and allows information to come to us so that we might consider our thoughts and actions. And when we find our thoughts and behavior in disagreement with His, we have the benefit of choice.

> No one can serve two masters; for either he will hate the one and love the other, or he will stand by and be devoted to the one and despise and be against the other. You cannot serve God and mammon [deceitful riches, money, possessions, or whatever is trusted in]. (Matthew 6:24, Amplified Version)

Don't Shoot The Messenger

Much of the information you will need to know about your "self" is sent and permitted through your spouse. When we conclude that our spouse is the problem, we forfeit vital information about our "self." The information we give up is essential to us intentionally participating with God. But some may ask, "What if my spouse is physically abusing me?"

Lauren had only been married to Joe for five months before verbal abuse turned physical. Lauren charged Joe's behavior to him having just lost his job, after a bitter dispute with his boss. Joe apologized and said that it would never happen again. But two months later it did. Again Lauren excused Joe's behavior because he was frustrated about still being unemployed. Still frustrated, Joe went out and got drunk. When he arrived home hungry and dinner was not ready, Joe exploded and beat Lauren. Lauren sympathized with Joe's pain, ignoring her own. She apologized and quickly prepared him something to eat. A few weeks later, Joe landed a job and things seemed to return to the pre-abuse state.

They were getting along well according to both Joe and Lauren. They had their first child. The first night Lauren and baby were home from the hospital, Joe initiated sex. Lauren was still experiencing discomfort from labor and delivery and therefore, declined. Joe hit the roof, punched a hole in the wall, pulled Lauren out of the bed onto the floor and began hitting her. Joe called her frigid and then suggested she was having an affair. Lauren managed to grab her cell phone off of the dresser and lock herself in the bathroom. She called the police. This was the first time she told Joe, "No!" It was this cry for help that landed Joe in jail with a court date. The judge ordered Joe to participate in anger management and for them to get marriage counseling. And this is how they ended up in our office.

It looks like Joe is Lauren's problem, right? If Joe would cease from verbally and physically abusing Lauren, then Lauren would be fine, right? Wrong! Lauren has a problem with boundaries. Her willingness to excuse Joe's behavior and remain in proximity, at the risk of her own life and availability to parent her child is unwise. Not only is it unwise to remain in range of someone that has proven to be out of control, we cannot find scripture to support such behavior. To the contrary, Jesus says this speaking of His life in John 10:18:

> No one takes it from me. I lay it down of my own free will. I have the right to lay it down; I also have the right to take it up again. I received this authority personally from my Father. ("The Message")

Counseling revealed Lauren derived her meaning from others. Early on, she learned how to make her father happy and win his approval—by conforming to his request and accepting responsibility for his faults. Lauren was well

58

trained by the time she married. Responding to Joe was natural. She was doing what she always did, only this time the stakes were higher.

Marriage is our last chance to grow up and become the person God intends. We grow up when our responses mirror God's. Lauren responded to Joe according to the way she was raised. God desired her to learn how to respond the way He made her. So is the problem of many that are married. Our responses reflect the way we were raised, rather than the way we were made. But, God doesn't give up on us. He will continue performing the work He began in us until Christ returns.

CHAPTER 6
IT'S AN INSIDE JOB!

"Conflict is GOD's request for something we have, in order that He can release more of Himself in us."

CONFLICT REQUIRES SOMETHING I have? We've all seen the spy movies in which there is a mole in the organization. A mole is someone on the inside of an organization that sells out to the enemy and attempts to bring the organization to its demise.

In the Matrix, the mole was Cypher. In Jesus' twelve, the mole was Judas. In your marriage, the mole is you! Now we know it is not a very welcomed or appealing thought that you could be the traitor in your marriage! But it is nonetheless true. When you got married, "you" entered into a covenant with God and your spouse. "You" entered into something God was doing--namely changing ad conforming His people into Christ's image. Friend, that change and conformity begins with you. "You" selected the spouse through whom you wanted to experience this process. God obliged with a spouse perfectly equipped and outfitted for the task. She is your helper. And not only so, but he serves her in this cause as well!

Self, not your spouse is the mole in marriage. Concerning your spouse, we might remember Romans 8: 28:

> And we know that all things work together for good to those who love God, to those who are the called according to *His* purpose.

This includes people. And that means our spouse. Yes, the hurt and pain they inflict work together to our benefit! Right after this in verse 29, Paul tells us that God's purpose for us is that we be conformed into the image of His Son. Our soul, that is our will and way of thinking are to reflect Christ in love and truth. This trumps all—pleasure, work, ministry, money, health, comfort, and convenience—all! And again, we say ALL!   Reader, it is the Purpose of purposes.   It is the Destiny of destinies to which each of us has been called. What conviction this must bring about in all we say and do in relationship to our spouse.

When we accept God's Purpose above all other purposes, including our individual purposes and destinies, then we can begin receiving all else from God toward this very end. God, our Father loves and cherishes us. He is committed to making us compatible for fellowship with Him, His Son and the Holy Spirit for eternity. This is the work He is doing in us and all that desire. Paul and Timothy wrote this to those in Christ Jesus who are in Philippi,

> I thank my God upon every remembrance of you, always in every prayer of mine making request for you all with joy, for your fellowship in the gospel from the first day until now, being confident of this very thing, that He who has begun a good work in you will complete *it* until the day of Jesus Christ; (Philippians 1: 3-6).

Knowing, believing and experiencing God's unconditional love for us will make it easier to face our own unloveliness. Pride prevents the best and most devoted followers of Christ from exposing ourselves. And because human nature rejects the unlovable, God provides the safety and sanctity of marriage relationship (and relationships formed in the body of Christ) to reveal our most unlovely parts. And He and those that truly know Him respond with unconditional love.

Faithful are His wounds, through whomever He allows them to be inflicted. He is our friend and open rebuke is better than secret love.

> Open rebuke is better than love carefully concealed. Faithful are the wounds of a friend, but the kisses of an enemy are deceitful. (Proverbs 27: 5, 6)

Self is marriage's number one private (and public) enemy! Inwardly, we resist being reduced to our lowest common denominator as husband and wife and that is, Christ Himself! Outwardly, we may be cooperative and true to the marriage process—but a slight survey or our motives by the Holy Spirit is likely to prove otherwise in nearly all. It's an inside job! Therefore, problems are a given!

No marriage is problem-free. In fact, it seems as soon as we resolve one problem a new one arises! Rick Warren, in an interview had this to say:

> Unresolved problems eventually result in conflict. This is because they must be solved, in order for them to cease. We have a problem until it is solved. While we may attempt many solutions, only the right one terminates the problem. The termination of a problem is also an invitation for a new one. We leave one problem to enter another. Disappointing, only when we feel that we have arrived, paid our dues and have outgrown the need for change.

Recently, we were told this story of our nephew. At eleven, in fifth grade, Cameron would routinely finish his math drills ahead of time and most others in his class. On idle, he would become playful with those still working. This would bring Cameron into conflict with his teacher. The teacher's solution was to give Cameron twice as many problems as the other students. The result was that repeating things he clearly knew bored Cameron and his playfulness continued. The conflict rose to involve his parents. Solution, give Cameron harder math problems. Cameron was tested to identify what kind of problems would challenge him. He got stuck at pre-algebra. Having determined the level of difficulty needed to challenge Cameron, the teacher began giving him pre-algebra problems during math drills. Cameron now had to interact with the teacher to learn how to master these knew problems. Result, Cameron stopped playing at inappropriate times. Conflict resolved. The right solution terminates the problem. And the termination of a problem is succeeded by a new problem. Read the words of Dr. Martin Luther King:

> All progress is precarious, and the solution of one problem brings us face to face with another problem.

Conflict Notifies Us

Conflict alerts the unknowing that there is a problem. When we are single, we generally do not consider our "self" to have a problem. We associate problems with things outside of us. And when we can't move them, we remove our "self." Sometimes, in doing so, key character flaws go unnoticed and consequently unaddressed. But it is not so easy to remove one's "self" from marriage. Marriage is a threefold chord: God, you and your spouse.

> Though one may be overpowered by another, two can withstand him. And a threefold cord is not quickly broken. (Ecclesiastes 4:12)

No fault divorce laws, online filing and all too eager attorneys promote quick and easy divorces. But there is nothing quick, easy or even painless about divorce. It's like taking a band-aid off that has bonded with a sore. It hurts! One reason is that God hates divorce. Read Malachi 2:16:

> For the LORD God of Israel says that He hates divorce, For it covers one's garment with violence, says the LORD of hosts. Therefore take heed to your spirit, that you do not deal treacherously.

The Message Translation words it this way:

> I hate divorce, says the GOD of Israel. GOD-of-the-Angel-Armies says, 'I hate the violent dismembering of the "one flesh" of marriage.' So watch yourselves. Don't let your guard down. Don't cheat.

From these verses, we can safely say that God is not in agreement with most divorces that occur. And although He honors our freedom to choose divorce, He does not lift the painful consequences associated with it. Unfortunately, unresolved conflict results in divorce for many, including Christians. This should not be so!

But before and even after divorce, God continues trying to contact us. Conflict is like someone ringing our cell phone. Cell phones are popular and personal, much more personal than our home or work phones. At home or work, the call could be for any number of people. But when our cell phone rings, we know it is for us. We are for whom the bell tolls. Conflict is God calling us on our cell phone. While we may not all have one, God still has our number. He knows how to get in touch with us. Refusal to respond doesn't stop God from calling, no more than the telephone marketing people stop when you don't answer. They just call back later. So does God. Unlike the sales calls that seek our money, God seeks our heart – our whole heart.

Two Opposing Wills

Conflict is two opposing wills and desires functioning in the same place at the same time. We wrongly assume these two wills and desires belong to husband and wife. That's because it's easier to believe what we can see, especially when we are untrained to believe and rely on what we cannot see. Paul encourages us this way:

> For our light affliction, which is but for a moment, is working for us a far more exceeding *and* eternal weight of glory, while we do not look at the things which are seen, but at the things which are not seen. For the things which are seen *are* temporary, but the things which are not seen *are* eternal. (II Corinthians 4:17, 18)

65

Now think this through with us. We already learned that all things are from God through God and to God in Romans 11:36. Then Colossians 1:16 - 17 informs us:

> For by Him all things were created that are in heaven and that are on earth, visible and invisible, whether thrones or dominions or principalities or powers. All things were created through Him and for Him. And He is before all things, and in Him all things consist.

And I Corinthians 15:28 tells us:

> Now when all things are made subject to Him, then the Son Himself will also be subject to Him who put all things under Him, that God may be all in all.

We can believe God will be all in all later or we can believe and receive Him as all and in all *now*. If we choose the latter, then how can the two opposing wills be your will and your spouse's will? If for us, God is all and in all, then the two wills in opposition must be His and ours! Perhaps this might strike a better chord with us if we remember that God's sole agenda is to make many sons and daughters in His image. Colossians 1:15 may further help establish this truth in our minds:

> He [Christ] is the image of the invisible God, the firstborn over all creation.

That Jesus Christ was the first-born implies that there are others. We who believe are those others! Romans 8:29 underscores this:

> For those whom He foreknew [of whom He was aware and loved beforehand], He also destined from the beginning [foreordaining them] to be molded into the image of His Son [and share inwardly His likeness], that He might become the firstborn among many brethren.

When we find our "self" in conflict, not only is our will in opposition to God's will, but also the stronger of these two wills is making a request of us. James 4 states clearly that conflict arises from our desires for (self) pleasure and (self) protection. Jesus did not live for pleasure, although He enjoyed life. Nor did Jesus try to protect Himself. We do both. And we are highly competent. Pleasure is anything that excites or thrills the mind and body. Self-protection has to do with providing for and preserving one's life.

God is asking for our desire to live. In Matthew 16, you may recall Peter challenging Jesus upon hearing Him speaking of to go to Jerusalem suffer many things and die. Jesus responded by exposing Satan origin of this thought. And then Jesus told Peter that his mind was not filled with the intentions of God. Jesus went further in verse 24 and explained that the desire to serve Him is incompatible with self.

> Then Jesus said to His disciples, 'If anyone desires to be My disciple, let him deny himself [disregard, lose sight of, and forget himself and his own interests] and take up his cross and follow Me cleave steadfastly to Me, conform wholly to My example in living and, if need be, in dying, also].' (Matthew 16: 24 Amplified Version)

Jesus was not saying that His disciples should make a list of all the things they shouldn't do! And neither should we as some suppose! Rather, He is informing them (and us) that in choosing Him—*the way He thinks and behaves,* they (and we) will at that same moment abandon self. This is because our human nature and its selfish tendency are in direct opposition to Divine Nature. Jesus committed to yielding His human nature to Divine Nature. Likewise, we each must commit.

Therefore, we must choose whom we will serve: God or self. This will always be the question before us: hour after hour, day after day, week in and week out until the day Christ returns! And though the thoughts, attitudes, behavior, people and things against which the choice is leveraged may change, the question remains: *Whom will you serve—God or self?*

God sends this same e-mail to all in His database. Albeit, the attachment that accompanies each is personal. God, the One that writes the question and hits "Send", also predetermines the attachment suitable for each. For this reason, opening the right one nearly always results in an intensely personal, painful, often humiliating revelation of self. That's why we prefer to read each other's mail and delete our own! Some deny they even received the e-mail! Commonly, we feel that we have to do everything, put up with everything and get nothing in return. Moreover, we feel godly in motive and delivery at best, and fulfilling our vow at least. Now imagine asking such a one, "Whom will you serve?" Is this really a question to one that believes he or she is serving God and fulfilling his or her vow? No, it's an insult and that's putting it mildly! How dare we be asked to do more! It's plainly rude and insensitive! After all, that pastor, counselor or co-worker doesn't know your spouse and all that he or she has put you through, right? Why do you have to be the "the one"? It's just not fair, is it?

While the attachments and requests they extend to each may be different, unequal and unfair: the sacrifice required of all is not! Christian, serving God is taking a life and giving a life! It's an exchange! Christ gave us His life through the cross. And we that believe give our life to Christ through that same cross! Marriage behaves likewise! Husband, wife: marriage is a life for a life—nothing more, nothing less. Recurring marital conflict is a good indication that we have not settled this truth. That is, we still have ways of thinking, feeling and behaving upon which we depend, prefer and choose over God.

68

Conflict Is God's Request

You have something and God desires it. He paid for it. We were bought by Christ's death and our life is not ours to do what we will. When we try and hold on to what is not ours, we challenge the owner to confront us. Try taking a bone out of a pit bull's mouth once giving it to him. You might very well be in the fight of your life! Although we give our life to Christ and might remember the date in which we did, we routinely take it back. Conflict is proof that we have either taken our life back or better still that there is life yet in us to give. Severe and prolonged struggles are two ways we become willing to offer our life to God.

> But we have this treasure in earthen vessels, that the excellence of the power may be of God and not of us. *We are* hard-pressed on every side, yet not crushed; *we are* perplexed, but not in despair; persecuted, but not forsaken; struck down, but not destroyed—always carrying about in the body the dying of the Lord Jesus, that the life of Jesus also may be manifested in our body. (II Corinthians 4:7-10)

Verse 16 adds this:

> Therefore we do not lose heart. Even though our outward man is perishing, yet the inward *man* is being renewed day by day.

Our most coveted natural resources are buried in the earth including gold, ore, diamonds and most other precious stones. They must be mined from the earth. In the same manner, the things about you that are most precious to God are buried beneath your physical beauty, your strengths and your gifts and even your greatest accomplishments. None of these things are "you." For your treasure is hidden within your earthen body. Our real worth to God is in who we are, not what we do.

When confronted, we typically answer with our strengths.

69

Ever notice that the very things that irritate you most about your spouse are the things in which you are most competent? Whenever we are operating in our strength, we see our spouse in their weakness. Perhaps unintentionally, we force our spouses into their weaknesses. When this happens and they feel exposed, some respond by attacking, others by being overly apologetic and still others by avoiding us all together.

Ron and Donna fought constantly. If he said, "Up," she said, "Down." If he said, "It was a mistake!" She said, "It was on purpose!" Donna said that she was unable to follow because Ron refused to lead. Ron fired back, "If she would follow I could lead!" According to Ron, the reason he didn't talk or get involved much at home was because Donna talked all the time and did everything. Donna was convinced that she talked a lot because he hardly talked at all. She admitted to doing most things around the house. But it was only because if she didn't, it wouldn't get done.

She was structured. He was unstructured. Only to Ron, she was controlling and he was relaxed. He wanted her to relax. She wanted him to work. This was the cycle of Ron and Donna's conflict! This seesaw way of responding in conflict will never bring resolution. It will result in many ups and downs for Ron and Donna and growing frustration.

Ron and Donna each had a problem revealed by conflict. While well informed about each other's problem, it was evident both were clueless concerning their own. They opened the wrong attachment. Ron and Donna were right about each other, but wrong about themselves. Failing to see their own condition, each was convinced the other was the cause and cure of their marital ills.

> Why do you see the speck that is in your brother's eye but do not notice or consider the beam [of timber] that is in your own eye? Or how can you say to your brother, Brother, allow me to take

out the speck that is in your eye, when you yourself do not see the beam that is in your own eye? You actor [pretender, hypocrite]! First take the beam out of your own eye, and then you will see clearly to take out the speck that is in your brother's eye. (Luke 6:41, 42)

These verses tell us how to approach this question of condemning in our spouse what we excuse in our "self." Read what it says:

A pupil is not superior to his teacher, but everyone [when he is] completely trained [readjusted, restored, set to rights, and perfected] will be like his teacher.

In other words, we should come to the question as a student and not one that has mastery. For also consider James' statement in chapter three, verse two:

For we all stumble in many things. If anyone does not stumble in word, he *is* a perfect man, able also to bridle the whole body.

A Chinese Proverb says, "Don't complain about the snow on your neighbor's roof when your own doorstep is unclean.

Can You Hear Us Now?

Repeated refusals to answer God result in Him using alternate methods and people to get our attention. Bob's wife Cindy had been telling him for sometime that he alienated his son by his harsh and critical attitude. Unfortunately, Bob thought sarcasm was a service rendered. She suggested that he plan regular bonding activities enjoyable to his son. Cindy felt that way their son would have a greater desire to comply with his father's requests and reduce feelings of intimidation. Bob, a military man, took his son camping and could not help but make a life lesson out of it. It was a disaster!

Several weeks later, Bob was called into his supervisor's office. Bob was told that although he was one of the most productive managers, his department was turning over workers at the same rate burgers are flipped at McDonalds. The company had already received several complaints and thus far successfully resolved them. But with so many complaints, the company feared being sued. So despite bringing in the most revenues, the company decided that any one lawsuit could strike a devastating financial blow. The risk of loss outweighed the gains Bob brought in. Bob was fired!

And surely, if wife, son and company have concerns about Bob's behavior then certainly there must be some validity in their experience of Bob. The people were different —Bob was the same. The circumstances were different—the problem the same. Bob was the common denominator! The problem was not someone on the outside trying to do Bob in. It was an inside job! Bob was doing himself in by failing to open the right e-mail attachment.

The regularity and strength of marital, family and work discord equaled the degree to which Bob resisted answering God. And so it is true with us: the frequency and intensity of marital conflict equals the degree to which we are unwilling to give God what He requests. So our spouse can never truly be our problem! Moreover, God says in Proverbs 16:7:

> When a man's ways please the LORD, He makes even his enemies to be at peace with him.

No peace? Consider your ways. Writer, Hamilton W. Mabie once said, "Nothing is lost upon a man who is bent upon growth; nothing wasted on one who is always preparing for life by keeping eyes, mind and heart open." And science fiction author, Lois Bujold gives this advice, "Examine what is said, not him who speaks."

Therefore says the LORD: If you return, Then I will bring you back; You shall stand before Me; If you take out the precious from the vile, You shall be as my mouth. Let them return to you, But you must not return to them. (Jeremiah 15:19)

One Sword, Two Edges

Conflict serves the purposes of God in both husband and wife. It is a two-edged sword designed to circumcise both husband and wife. The same argument asks different questions of each and therefore, requires different answers from each. Understanding what God is asking of us and giving it to Him ends conflict. We answer Him correctly when considering our own character flaws and their contribution to conflict. By taking responsibility for our weaknesses, we are then able to offer them to God. We cannot offer to God what we have not owned. Admitting our weaknesses is the beginning of owning them. But we must examine them thoroughly with God. And this only after we have offered our weaknesses to Him.

Blame, denial and minimizing are all ways we avoid taking ownership. But God will contend with us until all that remains is our utter weakness. Unfortunately, some of us have to literally lose everything to realize that God is the only thing there is. Rick Warren said, "You never know God is all you need until God is all you have."

Marriage has a way of bringing us to the end of our "self." Marriage is not satisfied until it gets life from you—all of your life! It is the unceasing, hostile dismembering of everything in us and about us that prevents oneness. Every thought, every attitude, every belief, every behavior—all: no matter how large or small, significant or insignificant, expensive or inexpensive, must be destroyed until there is One—God.

When our wrong thoughts, attitudes, beliefs and behavior are attached to things and people, they are subject to loss as well. There can only be One. This brings new meaning to Genesis 2:24:

> Therefore, a man shall leave his father and mother and be joined to his wife, and they shall become one flesh.

CHAPTER 7
PROBLEM HALF SOLVED
"The best response to conflict is to be honest about YOUR contribution."

WE HAVE ALL heard it said that a problem correctly defined is a problem half solved. Knowing we have a problem and outgrowing our need to blame our spouse for it positions us to obtain the answer. When a problem or need is correctly answered, it ceases to exist. Only then do we enter into a new problem to solve. Said another way, life is about asking and answering questions. While you are asking some, you are answering others. It happens simultaneously and is ongoing. But we only get to advance when we correctly answer the question, solving the problem at hand. Different partner, different church, different job and yet the same problem—we have offered the wrong answer. It's just that simple!

Now consider that a minister or justice of the peace blessed us on our wedding day and we felt the ripple effect of the blessing throughout the "honeymoon" period of marriage. The onset of conflict announces that the breaking process has begun. You'll recall Jesus' words in all four gospels and Paul repeating them in Corinthians:

> And as they were eating, Jesus took bread, blessed and broke it, and gave it to the disciples and said, 'Take, eat; this is My body.' (Matthew 26:26)

And then we learned that Jesus identified Himself as the Bread of Life in John 6:35. Just before this in verse 33, Jesus said:

> For the bread of God is He who comes down from heaven and gives life to the world.

Now consider that in John 3:3, in both the Amplified and Message translations of the Bible, we are told that unless we are born from above we can neither see nor experience what God has intended. Put this together with Jesus' prayer in John 17:11:

> I am no longer in the world, but these are in the world, and I come to You.

Verse 15 reads:

> I do not pray that You should take them out of the world, but that You should keep them from the evil one.

In these passages, we understand that Jesus declared Himself, "The Bread of Life." We learn that bread comes from above. And that whosoever is born of God is born from above. Now Jesus is no longer in the world, but we are and He has asked the Father not to take us out of the world but to keep us from the evil one. We are now the bread through whom Christ gives life to the world, beginning in our own homes. We are the bread of life that God intends to serve to our spouse. We were blessed.

Now we are being broken. Conflict is supposed to break us into edible pieces that can be served to our spouse. We wouldn't dare try giving a whole loaf of bread to an adult, much less a child. Yet, we attempt to give our spouse our substance all in one mouthful. When they spit us out due to nearly having choked, we think something is wrong with them. How many times has our spouse said, "Enough", "I don't like it" or "No more"? And then when they yell out, act out, or run out we want someone to come deal with him or her! They told us it was too much and they didn't like it. They showed us. And we still try to feed them huge uncooked, portions of food—that is, our strengths and way of doing things.

The problem is, the food hasn't been properly prepared and the portion size is too large. Think about it, there is only so much of some people we can take, right? Sometimes that person is our spouse! And for others, sometimes that person is us!

Dawn wanted Trevor to take more responsible actions by his own initiation. Each morning, Dawn asked Trevor his plans for the day. Trevor was routinely vague. This frustrated Dawn to no end because it generally meant low productivity for Trevor. Dawn decided to help Trevor by reviewing her "to do" list with him and suggesting he create one. She purchased him a planner from Franklin Covey, wrapped it and presented it to him. It was beautiful and manly, giving one the appearance of being well organized. Trevor promised to use it. And He did, for a couple of weeks, then he decided all that writing was not for him. When asked why he no longer carried it, Trevor told Dawn that writing was tedious.

Dawn had the answer—one of those hot new "smart phones" that double over as a planner with voice activated functions as well as a built in camera, video and voice recorder. No paper, no pens—certainly this was the answer. Dawn, being the resourceful and efficient one, researched the best one to buy and invested in one. She was helping Trevor get organized and she was only too delighted.

Trevor never took the "smart phone" out of the box! It sat for almost a year. Dawn was angry. She said that it was because she spent a lot of money on the "smart phone" to help Trevor and she thought he could have at least tried it. To make matters worse, Trevor had told her that he knew he needed to become more organized. However, he had become increasingly resentful of her demands and attempts to make him conform to her way of doing things. He experienced her motivations as self-serving.

At first, Trevor responded the way she wanted him to, with no conviction to follow through. In fact, he didn't see his disorganization as the mammoth sized problem Dawn made it to be. After all, Dawn maximizes everything! Certainly, she was over-exaggerating this too! Okay, he's lost a few high paying jobs because of his failure to meet deadlines. The people person he was, Trevor could talk his way into the president's office if need be. His form and style were flawless. However, his substance left something to be desired.

Dawn's answer—get all the substance in at one serving, or at least as much as possible, as fast as possible to get Trevor up to speed. Dawn was neither mindful of the quality of the food, nor the fact that Trevor grew up learning to dislike this kind of food; add this to serving the wrong portion size and Trevor's real need for the food and we have one big problem! Excuse us; we should say that Dawn had a problem. Better still, we should say Dawn and Trevor each had a problem. And the problem is not each other, for our spouse can never be our problem! We use the first letters of each word in the phrase, "Your Spouse Is Not Your Problem" to convey this concept to couples. Here it is:
Your **SIN** Your **P**roblem!

Both Sinned

Trevor and Dawn's sin is self-preservation that has its origin in pride. Dawn, demanding Trevor become more organized and disciplined, ensured her survival and security while she remained essentially unchanged. Her gifts were self-serving and secondarily about Trevor. Because they were joined in spirit and both of their souls cherished their own way, Trevor rightly discerned Dawn's impure motive. It threatened what he cherished. But not only did Trevor cherish his way, he relied on it, as it made him very

78

successful as an unmarried man. However, now married all contributed to his demise and their relationship challenges.

The same was true for Dawn. She was equally devoted, dependent and successful as an unmarried woman. Both Trevor and Dawn were committed, albeit to self rather than God or each other. Each attempted tp prolong his or her self life, while wanting to believe and convey it as the "Christian Life." The more each pressed the other to change, the more resistant the other became. This tug of war went on for a long time. Each refused to let go of his and her life—his and her way of thinking and behaving. Christian, read what Jesus, in Matthew 16:25 - 26, has to say about this approach to life:

> For whoever is bent on saving his [temporal] life [his comfort and security here] shall lose it [eternal life]; and whoever loses his life [his comfort and security here] for My sake shall find it [life everlasting]. For what will it profit a man if he gains the whole world and forfeits his life [his blessed life in the kingdom of God]? Or what would a man give as an exchange for his [blessed] life [in the kingdom of God]?

In the last chapter we discussed Matthew 16:23 and 24. Do you remember Peter was standing in Jesus' way? Peter forced Jesus to make a decision about the route He would take. Jesus didn't stop or swerve around Peter. He expected a collision and did not try and avoid it! Jesus responded by telling him (Satan) to get out of His way. Trevor and Dawn did not share each other's way. Moreover, neither shared God's way of thinking and behaving in relationship to the other. So while each may have felt right and justified in his and her own eyes, the outcome was undesirable for both! Conflict, and especially recurring conflict has a way of convincing every married couple of this profundity.

Like Peter and Jesus, and Trevor and Dawn; we do not share our spouse's manner and way. This is partly responsible for our attraction to one another. But it is also a great source of irritation to each of us. Our differences offer us opportunities to engage in the work of considering other ways of doing things. It's fun at first because there is no requirement and thus pressure. We just like to be together. It feels good and good things usually happen. Yet, selfishness safely flies below radar, going virtually undetected! But conflict sifts out the most cleverly concealed devotion to self. If that is not enough, recurring conflict will reveal the most pious attempts of self to resist, submit and genuinely participate in the process of change.

James Allen in his book, "As A Man Thinketh" writes, "The man who cannot endure to have his errors and shortcomings brought to the surface and made known but tries to hide them, is unfit to walk the highway of truth."

Letting Go

It is in letting go of what we value that we grant opportunity to our spouse to take what they need. Dawn, letting go of the need to control by structuring, organizing and formalizing all, would make these wonderful traits available to Trevor to take as he wills. And with a little help from God to influence Trevor toward this end, Trevor has the greatest opportunity to choose to live more organized. Remember, God wants what Dawn wants for Trevor for different reasons. Dawn desires to protect her life. God desires Trevor to allow more of this mind and manner of Christ to dwell within Him. And just what does God think concerning planning as it relates to provision:

> You lazy fool, look at an ant. Watch it closely; let it teach you a thing or two. Nobody has to tell it what to do. All summer it stores up food; at harvest it stockpiles provisions. So how long are you going to laze around doing nothing? How long before you get out of bed? A nap here, a nap there, a day off here, a day off there, sit back, take it easy—do you know what comes next? Just this: You can look forward to a dirt-poor life, poverty your

permanent houseguest! (Proverbs 6:6-11, "The Message")

Think God is on Dawn's side on this one? We think so too! However, Dawn just needs to turn over the car keys to God and allow Him to drive from here on! When she realizes that apart from God, her best efforts will continue to fail to produce outcomes desirable to God, Trevor and self, Dawn may become more willing to relinquish the keys that drive her heart. Dawn has what God needs. Conflict dislodges and exposes our sinful motives. And the motives we need to focus on are our own, rather than our spouses.

When in conflict, we can simply ask God to show us our motivations, agree with God and then accept His way of cleansing them and serving them to our spouse. Until we do, we will revisit the same conflict over and over again. It serves a purpose and until we retire its purpose by examining our own motives, we can neither enter the cleansing process nor expect God to change our spouse. Two scriptures might help here:

> If we say that we have no sin, we deceive ourselves, and the truth is not in us. If we confess our sins, He is faithful and just to forgive us *our* sins and to cleanse us from all unrighteousness. If we say that we have not sinned, we make Him a liar, and His word is not in us" (I John 1:8-10)

But some will say, "Surely my sin is not as bad as my spouse's." Paul advises us that it is not wise to compare our "self" to one another in II Corinthians 10:12. Some will always seem to look better than us and others will always seem to look worse than us. When we want to feel good about our "self," we can compare our self against those who appear worse off. And when we don't feel so good about our "self," we can always find those that seem better off. But do such exercises change you or your spouse for that matter?

> For the weapons of our warfare *are* not carnal but mighty in God for pulling down strongholds, casting down arguments and every

81

high thing that exalts itself against the knowledge of God, bringing every thought into captivity to the obedience of Christ, and being ready to punish all disobedience when your obedience is fulfilled. (II Corinthians 10:4-6)

We battle an unseen enemy. And "self" is one of the most destructive weapons in his arsenal! When we fulfill our personal responsibility to God, then we are ready to rebuke others. Only then will we have developed so much love and compassion for others that God will literally have to move us to rebuke. And if and when we do, it is with such great love and concern for others welfare, rather than for our own preservation.

Resolving Conflict

The quickest way to begin resolving conflict is to take your sticks out of the fire! Christian, it is required. If only half remains for the fire to consume, then the fire will go out a whole lot quicker. For some, half might be a generous number of sticks; for others, half may be less. Short of God, there's really no way of telling how significant our contribution is to reaching resolve. But once removed, the healing can begin. However, we do know that the contents of a can labeled "flammable" under specified conditions, does not explode unless those conditions are met. Conflict is proof the conditions have been met. Removing our part causes the fire to go out. While it might flicker awhile, it must go out.

Deep communication and sharing, in love of course, about our spouse's weaknesses and the pain inflicted upon us are important, but they will not resolve conflict. Let us say this again, as it bears repeating. Focusing on our spouse's weaknesses and the trouble they have caused, no matter how great the insult, will not resolve conflict. Try this if you must, but sooner or later Christian, you will come back to these words. Why do we say this? This is a good place for a review and a helpful one at that.

God has how many agendas? One! What is God's agenda? His agenda is to transform us into the image of Jesus Christ. That is to change our character and related thoughts, attitudes, beliefs and behaviors into His. The goal is that we have the mind of Christ, as Paul instructs us in Philippians 2:5 - 7:

> Let this mind be in you which was also in Christ Jesus, who, being in the form of God, did not consider it robbery to be equal with God, but made Himself of no reputation, taking the form of a bondservant, *and* coming in the likeness of men.

Aside from this, think about how many times you have already "shared your heart," confronted or just retreated and resigned from your spouse's weaknesses. Most of us have employed these methods; some of us for years and the problem is still present. Even those that divorce and remarry eventually discover that the problems they strongly believed were their spouse's show up again. The face may change, but the problem remains the same! Who might we ask is the common denominator? Wherever you go—there you are!

Conflict Announces Division

When there is conflict, there is division. The division is between God and us—that is, each spouse is disconnected in some manner from God. We are disconnected in the area in which we refuse to respond to God. Most of us have experienced a piece of a patch or appliqué tear from the garment to which it was applied. A good part of the appliqué and garment are still intact, but the torn piece needs to be sewn again to the garment. Our unlovable parts are like these patches that need to be reapplied to the garment. God desires all of us, all of our unlovely parts, as well as our lovable parts, to be securely in relationship with Him. When the patch is sewn back in place, we can say the garment has been restored. When we own, offer and allow God to cleanse our unlovable parts and impure motives and then give them to Him in full view of our spouse, the healing begins.

You see, whatever remains out of relationship cannot be healed. And where there is a divide between husband and wife, there needs to be a bridge. More communication, deeper communication—merely sending messages back and forth does not guarantee a bridge. In fact, what many of us have come to realize is that no matter how sincere the effort, going over everything again and again seems to create more confusion. The more we talk, the more we feel compelled to rationalize our behavior at the expense of our spouse.

Once before said, albeit still amusing, is that what we find excusable in ourselves, we find condemnable in our spouse. It's all a matter of perception. And we each are entitled to our own, right? Stay with yours if you wish, but if you have ever felt devastated by your spouse's behavior at some point, you must consider what lies within you that is either so proud or misinformed that could have allowed for such emotional destruction.

Disappointment, devastation and destruction are not only feelings we experience in relationship to what happens or who happens outside of us. These feelings attack and expose egos in hiding. In his book, "Letters to a Devastated Christian," Gene Edwards provides God's would-be servant some guidelines for overcoming the devastation of what has happened to him. On page 88, he writes, "First of all, you need to search your own heart and realize that a great deal of the problem lies with your own psychological make-up."

And concerning the ego, Edwards writes, "You need to remember that you fell for the appeal that you were special. At one time you felt exalted in that when you heard this word it fed something within your nature." And that you are disheartened and reproved by the same suggests that what was initially fed had less to do with God and a whole lot more to do with "self."

British Novelist, Iris Murdock once wrote, "People often start by falling in love, and they go on for years without realizing that that love must change into some other love which is so unlike it that it can hardly be recognized as love at all." The kind of love you displayed while dating and even while honeymooning must change.

Don't Get Us Wrong

Your spouse does have a problem! There are things inside of your spouse that God wants out so that He can replace them with responsible or relational love. God simply has not delegated the assignment to you! So, when you remove your contribution, God is free to deal with your spouse. With our "stuff" out of the way, nothing now stands between God and our spouse.

But it's hard for us to stay out of the way, isn't it? We see clearly what is wrong with our spouse. And God agrees. It seems like God is taking forever to change your spouse. You've been waiting a long time! And you are tired by now—frustrated—maybe even ready to give up. Thankfully, God can count on the millions of moments we have resisted yielding to Him and He has not given up on us. These are moments when we hold onto our life, our strengths and our resources. We consume them upon our "self," rather than letting go and allowing God to distribute them as He wills. No new life is generated; therefore, death and decay result.

But the wise spouse understands and accepts all things from God—for the purpose of exposing and rooting out evil and establishing Christ's character in him or her. Wise spouses use their partner's unchanged thoughts, attitudes and behaviors to aid them in seeing and responding the way God would have them. We need more of what our spouse has, minus the impurity of their motives. A wise husband or wife understands Jeremiah 15:19:

> Therefore thus says the Lord [to Jeremiah]: If you return [and give up this mistaken tone of distrust and despair], then I will give you again a settled place of quiet and safety, and you will be My minister; and if you separate the precious from the vile [cleansing your own heart from unworthy and unwarranted suspicions concerning God's faithfulness], you shall be My mouthpiece. [But do not yield to them.] Let them return to you-- not you to [the people].

You have heard it said, "It takes two to tango!" Both husband and wife together trigger reactions in each other that God desires to address. We each bring something to conflict. The quickest way to diffuse conflict is to take ownership for our own stuff. If you haven't figured it out by now, you and your spouse come from two different worlds, or so it seems. Yet, it's not really two different worlds, but rather two different realities. It is so common that husbands

husbands and wives are born into and raised in competing realities that we might it consider it a stroke of genius!

CHAPTER 8
LET'S BE HONEST!

"Honesty does not relieve us of our responsibility to uphold the marriage vow we made to GOD."

WHILE HONESTY MAY provide us with initial and necessary relief, the relief is only temporary. Honesty is not necessarily the same as truth. Honesty cleanses us, but it is truth that heals us. We can be honest about what we think and feel, but this does not make it automatically true. Brenda thought John committed adultery because there was something wrong with her. She felt inferior and thus insecure at the idea of not measuring up or being enough for John. Despite being hurt and angry with John, she made excuses for his sin.

Brenda told us honestly what she thought and felt upon hearing of John's affair. Brenda took responsibility for John's sin because she felt insecure in relationship to John. However, in James 1, we are told the truth about the origin of sin:

> Don't blame God when you are tempted! God cannot be tempted by evil, and He doesn't use evil to tempt others. We are tempted by our own desires that drag us off and trap us. Our desires make us sin, and when sin is finished with us, it leaves us dead. (Contemporary English Version)

The truth is, that John's sin arose from his own 'internal' desires. Brenda was honest with us in telling us she believed John's adultery was her fault. But Brenda was honestly wrong! Brenda believed a lie. However, the lie was not as dangerous as the place it held in her heart. Brenda not only believed she was at fault, she behaved this way, too. Brenda constantly made personal adjustments to accommodate John. This was her responsibility, or so she thought. Unfortunately, none of the adjustments Brenda made seemed to influence John to behave differently toward her.

In fact, John seeing her willingness to accept responsibility for his shortcomings made blaming her easy. Brenda was stuck. She loved John, but was tired and felt powerless in relationship with him. John's constantly changing, self-defined needs resulted in an appetite impossible for any one person to satisfy. He became increasingly demanding and verbally abusive.

God's truth had already prevailed against the lie that another human being could make John sin. John's internal desires drove him to commit adultery. But Brenda still maintained the freedom to choose whether or not she would believe this or hold onto her original belief—in which she was at fault. Unfortunately, it did not help Brenda that John blamed her lack of interest in him sexually as the reason for his behavior. Had John outgrown his need for blame, Brenda might have gained more immediate support and the confidence she needed to replace the lie with truth.

However, since adultery was the reason they decided to take the Radical Love course in the first place, Brenda did receive the help she needed to establish her identity in Christ, rather than in John. Brenda began looking to God for meaning in life and relationships. John was both attracted and repelled by Brenda's newfound freedom in Christ. He expressed interest in taking the course a second time—this time for him! The first time he took it, he told us that it was for her.

Honesty Cleanses Us

Honesty cleanses and prepares the soul for healing, but it is truth that actually heals the soul. All of her life, Brenda took responsibility for others. So it is no wonder that she found it easy to take responsibility for John's sin. She was doing what she had always done! It was natural to her. And though taking on the burdens of others as her own contributed to her feeling terrible about herself, Brenda thought it her duty. After all, she was a Christian taught to bear other's burdens.

Scripture does teach this, however, not to the detriment of who we are. Brenda could not have been motivated by love; she felt guilty about not being able to supply her husband's sexual desires. Guilt inspired behavior is not the same as love inspired behavior. Guilt is the awareness of having done something wrong. It is often accompanied by shame, regret and fear of reprisal. Shame has to do with who we are and regret is the sadness we feel for being wrong and causing harm to others. Fear is a spirit. Most experience it as worry, anxiety, or panic when we cannot control potentially negative outcomes.

Brenda was dependent on John financially and emotionally. She feared abandonment. So, Brenda accepted his cruel behavior and unkind words—she thought she had to for provision's sake. In the Book of Lamentations, we find the people of God doing exactly the same thing:

> We have had to pay money to drink the water that belongs to us; our [own] wood is sold to us. Our pursuers are upon our necks [like a yoke]; we are weary and are allowed no rest. We have given the hand [as a pledge of fidelity and submission] to the Egyptians and to the Assyrians [merely] to get food to satisfy [our hunger]. Our fathers sinned and are no more, and we have borne their iniquities. Servants and slaves rule over us; there is none to deliver us out of their hands. We get our bread at the peril of our lives because of the sword of the wilderness [the wild Arabs, who may attack if we venture into the fields to reap our harvests]. (Amplified Version)

Here we observe a wounded people paying someone else for what God had already provided. Like God's people in the

Book of Lamentations, Brenda trusted man more than she trusted God. She was more afraid of being cut off by man than by God.

In Matthew 10:28, Jesus tells his disciples this:

> And do not fear those who kill the body but cannot kill the soul. But rather fear Him who is able to destroy both soul and body in hell.

In "The Message" reads this way:

> Don't be bluffed into silence by the threats of bullies. There's nothing they can do to your soul, your core being. Save your fear for God, who holds your entire life--body and soul—in his hands.

God will not be able to fully use Brenda to influence John until she relinquishes her need for him. As long as she needs him, she cannot lead him. Brenda will have to become completely dependent upon God for meaning and provision. In order for this to happen, she will have to give up her way of doing things. Even though it may be hard for her to see, Brenda's way is self-serving. Most that are dependent upon others do not see their behavior as self-serving because actions appear to serve others.

Brenda must recognize the error in placing her trust in man over God. Furthermore, she must distinguish her approach as self-serving, rather than God serving. It is a form of pride. Brenda must ask and receive forgiveness from God, let go of any and all that have sown or watered seeds of self-serving dependency upon others, also known as pride. By so doing, Brenda is cleansed from sin and the guilt and shame that accompany sin. Cleansing prepares Brenda for healing. Healing comes by receiving truth and obeying God.

Healed By Truth And Obedience

Though much has been accomplished, Brenda is not out of the woods yet. The cleansed area of her soul must be wrapped with bandages of truth. The muscles involved in the wounded area need to be rehabilitated. And then weight will have to be applied to build the muscle. All of this must take place in the gymnasium of her fear of re-injury. Like Brenda, the suffering encountered in marriage exposes our weaknesses. Admission and honesty during suffering cleanses us. Eugene Petersen, author of the Message Bible Translation tells us in I Peter 4:1 and 2 that suffering loosens our insistence on doing things our own way.

> Since Jesus went through everything you're going through and more, learn to think like him. Think of your sufferings as a weaning from that old sinful habit of always expecting to get your own way. Then you'll be able to live out your days free to pursue what God wants instead of being tyrannized by what you want. (I Peter 4: 1, 2 Message Translation)

Bandages are wrapped around injuries to provide cover and support during healing and rehabilitation. Imagine having a cast from hand to forearm. The wrist involved has limited mobility. Movement is restricted on purpose to ensure healing and full restoration. While it is awkward, uncomfortable and perhaps even embarrassing, we tolerate it for our ultimate good. Once the cast is off, we still must re-establish the use of hand and wrist. The more severe the injury, the more help we will need during recovery.

In the same manner, the bandage of truth must be wrapped around emotional wounds to protect and aid in healing and recovery. Truth restricts movement. It is designed to promote healing. Ultimately, God's desire is that truth be internalized and alone govern behavior. But before this happens, in almost all cases, God will assign someone (whether husband, or wife, or another) to be the bearer and banner of truth in the area of our weakness. Oftentimes, it is when we begin questioning their motives rather than receiving the truth they bring us that we both identify and discount the spouse assigned to deliver God's truth to us. We can dislike him or her, challenge the pureness of his or her motives, but none of this alters the truth they bring us. Jeremiah 15:18 - 21 reads:

> Why is my pain perpetual and my wound incurable, refusing to be healed? Will you indeed be to me like a deceitful brook, like waters that fail and are uncertain? Therefore thus says the Lord [to Jeremiah]: If you return [and give up this mistaken tone of distrust and despair], then I will give you again a settled place of quiet and safety, and you will be My minister; and if you separate the precious from the vile [cleansing your own heart from unworthy and unwarranted suspicions concerning God's faithfulness], you shall be My mouthpiece. [But do not yield to them.] Let them return to you--not you to [the people].

John was both Brenda's betrayer and her bandage. Brenda expressed feeling John's refusal as resistance to improving the quality of their relationship. Although discouraged by this, we suggested to Brenda that this was just the kind of resistance needed to develop the muscles of unconditional love! And that if she continued to look at her marriage as a partnership of equalities, it would not be long before she decided it was not and look for another more equal partner. She agreed. John betrayed Brenda by committing adultery. His refusal to accept responsibility for his behavior served as a bandage.

From the time she was a young girl, blame and irresponsibility resulted in Brenda assuming responsibility as well as the burden to "fix" it. And since she could not control those causing her pain, she adapted to their whims, wants and needs to relieve the pain. However, marriage taught Brenda a new reality: relieving the symptoms of pain and removing the cause of pain are entirely different.

92

Brenda still could not control John's behavior and adjusting to his whims and needs was ineffective. Brenda had the same problem she had while growing up! Instead of taking responsibility for her "self," she was still trying to take responsibility for others. Her response, then, was no longer acceptable to God now. God desired that Brenda grow up. She would have to adopt Christ's mind, in exchange for her own.

> Therefore My Father loves Me, because I lay down My life that I may take it again. No one takes it from Me, but I lay it down of Myself. I have power to lay it down, and I have power to take it again. This command I have received from My Father. (John 10:17-19)

As Christ, Brenda has the ability to give her life and take it back again. This commandment we receive from the Father. The only power John has over her life is that which she chooses to give him.

> Blessed *be* the LORD my Rock, Who trains my hands for war, and my fingers for battle. (Psalm 144:1)

Experience has been a wonderful teacher for Brenda up until this point. In many ways, she advanced to adulthood, complete with the skills and abilities necessary to fulfill her God-given purpose in life. But to actually fulfill His will for her life, from here on out, Brenda will have to allow God to be her teacher. She will have to lay down all that has faithfully served as weapons protecting her against emotional death and destruction. Brenda must learn how to depend on God, rather than the mercy of people. People certainly have been to helpful to Brenda. But also, they have been fleeting and unreliable. In no other relationship has this become more apparent to her than in marriage. Initially depending on God for emotional and physical support will be hard. Brenda brings years of training and reinforcement in trusting others to the task of trusting God over all. It will require intentional, persistent effort on

Brenda's part. But not always! It will become easier and easier. The day will come when Brenda mindlessly and naturally responds to God in the presence of her husband and all others, including their objections! Marriage is our last chance to grow up and become mature men and women reflecting God in all that we say and do.

Being honest pre-qualifies us for the truth we need to grow up. Brenda became pre-qualified. Understanding that we can be honest, yet honestly wrong, strengthens our eligibility for truth. Submitting her honesty to another at the risk of it being wrong in light of God's truth, strengthened Brenda's capacity to receive it. She was in a position to hear truth. Desire and faith enable us to hear truth. Upon coming to us, Brenda heard truth. Subsequent sessions confirmed that Brenda understood what she heard. She began talking about her relationship with John differently. Brenda spoke of her pain differently. She began behaving differently. Brenda even looked different! Brenda was different! She was armed with new information, practical skills and the ability to recognize opportunities to employ them in marriage. And she found a grander reason than John for doing so: it is what God desired of her. Brenda was determined to love John unconditionally because that is the way she had been loved by God. To Brenda, it both meant and ensured her freedom, while winning John his own. She could do this because it had been done for her. God unconditionally loved her and she knew it!

Brenda was more committed to the covenant she made with God and John than ever before. John could no longer take her life without permission. She offered her life to God for John's benefit. God was changing Brenda from the inside out. She loved John more deeply than ever, but he did not experience her behavior as loving. Brenda was closer to him than she had ever been, but John could not perceive it. He

94

was still being dishonest. He had not yet been pre-qualified for truth.

Brenda was in it with John, but no longer controlled by John. This is the place in which Jesus walked after He was crucified, died and rose from the dead, before ascending to the Father. It was the space between restoration and receiving a new body. Outwardly, Brenda looked the same to John. But, she had been internally transformed into the image of God! And what is God's objective but to change us back into His image.

Paul Eldrige, educator and novelist, states, "In the spider-web of facts, many a truth is strangled." Admitting the facts about our "self," whether glorious or gross, untangles the web of deceit responsible for sticking husbands and wives in opposing positions. The positions we take are based on the beliefs we hold. Invalid beliefs are far more hazardous to truth, than the lies from which they originate. We are told that Satan is the Father of lies. God overcame Satan by the cross. Truth overcame lies at the same place. But overcoming invalid beliefs requires our cooperation."

Brenda overcame her invalid beliefs. She was fit to walk on the highway of truth because Brenda was willing to have her errors in thinking and ineffective coping methods examined in the presence of another. Brenda did not try to hide her behavior, defend it, or minimize it by clinging to deceptively altruistic motives.

And what did she ultimately receive in exchange? Brenda received God's unconditional love, forgiveness, divine aid, and a peace that only those that experience it can understand. Brenda did not simply get relief from pain— she was delivered from pain all together. John could no longer hurt her. She was free to love John unconditionally. And more than desiring John to be a husband to her, Brenda desired his freedom from bondage. She couldn't leave him—who else would care enough, love enough, pray enough, be there enough for him to also gain this wonderful freedom. Brenda felt responsible, since she independently made a vow to God when she said, "I do." But it had become more than a responsibility, it was her desire!

Eventually, John made a 180-degree turnaround in the way He viewed God, his wife and family. He voluntarily admitted having sex with other women. John expressed sadness and deep remorse for the pain he caused Brenda. He vehemently refused to admit that he had told a lie or two in the process of committing adultery. Instead, John confessed to being a liar and that he had been one his entire life. John lied when the truth would not have resulted in trouble to him or others. He summed it up this way, "Liars, lie. That's who they are and that's what they do. They don't need a reason. I didn't need a reason. I just lied. I was a liar!" We ended the session with the four of us praying. We held hands and prayed silently while John offered his petition aloud with tears: "God make me a truth filled man: truthful in thought and true in my words and in my behavior. Also God, be aggressive with me in this that I might be true through and through. This I desire for me, God that I might truly reflect you in all and to all. This was gutsy, real and unfeigned. We sat in silence for the next few minutes and ended the session.

John confided in Brenda, and later to us that he was afraid of being abandoned by those he loved. For John, telling the truth meant punishment—to your room or to be left home by yourself. And he hated the idea of being left and feeling alienated and alone! So John played hide and seek for much of their 10-year marriage. He hid from his fear of Brenda leaving him by lying and appearing irresponsible and needy (*although in the beginning he strongly disagreed with each*). The antidote to the morbid feelings of being alone and inadequate was to seek pleasure through sex. John admitted that he didn't know how to be any different, until he began noticing Brenda gradually changing before his eyes. And while it did stop him from sin initially, the constancy of her love was captivating enough to offer John hope that one day he too could change for the better. So he kept stealing looks at her, and pretended not to be moved by the change that he was witnessing.

We all were surprised by the swiftness in which God moved in bringing John to godly sorrow and repentance. In the beginning, John was hopeless. Brenda was hoping and we were hopeful. God used each of us where we were to make something wonderful happen in this marriage! Today, John and Brenda continue their journey into what it truly means to become one in Christ. Each is claiming his and her life: the good, the bad and the ugly and offering all to God in exchange for His Son's Life. They still struggle. As their respective lives diminish the offerings become increasingly more valuable and more costly to give to the Lord.

But more and more often they report sharing with one another deeply and intimately about things they never would have imagined and in places and ways that words have failed them. In Christ, they are discovering God's Life. God has always desired to share it and that many would accept His invitation: Jesus Christ was first, then us—individually. It usually takes one spouse to enter and experience this Life first, before the other. And before you ask, 'No ladies, husbands do not need, nor are they required to go first.' Now it is nice and refreshing to my (Kim) feminine fancy and liking, but ladies not mandatory!

John and Brenda, like so many other couples have and are discovering, God's Life—*the Divine Life*. All that have will agree: God's Life is infinitely more attractive, adventurous and awe-inspiring than any of their own! It is a jaw-dropping experience! We really do get the better end of the deal!

We often encounter this Life through conflict. But most do not recognize it as a secret entrance into other rooms in God's house. You see, conflict gives us an opportunity to be honest with self, about self in relationship to God's truth concerning us—all in the presence and with the help of our spouse! Honesty is necessary if we are ever to gain receipt of the truth. Conflict allows us to wrestle with our reality in light of God. Many of our perceptions, which constitute a large part of our reality, are based on human nature and tendencies. Human nature has been laced with sin.

Now Christian husband and wife, God has already judged and forgiven every sin you will commit up until the day you die. Jesus Christ will not be judged again for them and neither will you. It's like gravity. It has worked, is working and will continue to work here on the earth until God determines otherwise. This is true whether or not we know, believe or accept it. We both benefit and have been hurt by gravity. It didn't change, nor does it: we did and we do! We either work with it or we are working against it. But we are always interacting with gravity here on earth. None escape its power or influence.

Similarly, by virtue of the Cross of Christ, your sins are forgiven you. This is true whether or not you believe it and accept it. The crucifixion of Christ occurred and was accepted by God as payment in full for sin. God didn't require our counsel or collaboration in establishing and meting out the judgment for sin. According to Roman 5: 8, God, Christ and the Holy Spirit accomplished all while we practiced sin! It is finished and complete as the judgment against sin having been satisfied.

Going forward will, however, require your participation. Realizing the freedom, love, authority and power available to you in your day-to-day, personal life and marriage is contingent upon you. Like John and Brenda and all others that would experience God's Life here on earth, you must get free from the lies and faulty beliefs left in the wake of sin. Some of the wake of sin includes: lies, impure motives, needs, hurt, pain and fear.

Sustaining freedom from sin's aftermath is proportionate to the degree of responsibility you accept for who you are and who you will choose to be in relationship with your spouse and others. There can be no freedom without personal responsibility. And without freedom and responsibility you cannot experience God's Life as intended. And this is true no matter how many scriptures we can quote, how many souls we introduce to Christ and no matter how eloquent or persuasive our words. Money, position, possessions are all irrelevant here. We need freedom to choose Christ's Life. We need responsibility to own and offer our thoughts, feelings, attitudes and way of doing things to Christ and accept to His thoughts and ways in exchange.

To the one that is free and responsible, nothing is wasted. Not one lie told us by our spouse, not one, two, three, four or more incidents of infidelity, not once being called out of name, not one thing that is added or taken from us against our will; no, not one thing will be wasted upon this one. All provides an experience that solicits a response. And how we respond: in word, deed and even more importantly in heart provides valuable feedback and insight as to our own progress in the journey of transformation into the image of Christ. If this is God's sole purpose and our pursuit, then all will, and must work together for our good toward this end. Moreover, God pre-selected, chose, set us apart for Christ's indwelling and equipping to respond to Him in all.

This all that love Him do vigorously until Christ comes. Will you husband? Will you wife?

CHAPTER 9
FREED TO SET OTHERS FREE

"The very best gift you can give your spouse is the freedom to be who he/she is, even though his/her behavior does not conform to what you think is right, what you know is right and what you know pleases GOD."

ONE OF THE most liberating experiences I (Kim) have had was in college. There, I met Diane, who to this day is familiarly called "Ecko" by friends. Ecko was two years my senior and clearly more learned than I. However, we both enjoyed philosophy. One time she told me about flowers, saying that each one needs a time, place and space to bloom. She went on to say people are like that. All require time. All require a place and space to happen, with the only response being love and truth. It sounded like an amazingly wonderful experience for the recipient. But who does that for another without wanting something in return? We were not Christian. Albeit, even today I don't know many truly unconditionally loving Christians! Nevertheless, Ecko determined to be so for me. The rules were simple. She asked the questions—especially questions beginning with "why." My part was to be honest, hers (in addition to asking the questions) to be a mirror and unconditionally accepting.

Carl Rogers, a psychologist, refers to this as "unconditional positive regard." But it was more than positively regarding me at all times; there were (and still are) times when my honesty opposes God's truth. When this occurred, Ecko would acknowledge my honesty, then she would almost always follow up with one of these "why" questions to give me the opportunity to reconcile my point of view with the truth. When it became obvious that I could not, she cleverly introduced a new viewpoint for my consideration. Ecko gave me permission to be me and challenged me to become the best me possible. She would say that if I spent my life trying to be someone else, then who would be "me." It made sense to me. This was a wonderful and truly unforgettable way of learning for me. Ecko showed me how to value another's reality, by first acknowledging my own.

I experienced freedom. I wanted others to have it. I desired to give this experience to others. No greater gift can a husband give a wife and a wife a husband, than the freedom to be who he or she is, even when it costs him or her everything. This is marriage—a life for a life!

When we come to the resolve that our spouse 'knowing God' is eternally more important than our present fulfillment, then our rights, desires and dreams become expendable. Marriage is designed to bring us to this place. It is here that we become willing to let go of what we think is right, may know is right and what pleases God. Our own opinions become less important to us while pleasing God begins to matter more. And do you know how long God has been waiting for us to arrive at this place? Suffice it to say, a very long time! And He is willing to wait our entire life in need be.

Mother May I?

There was a game we played as children called, "Mother May I? In it there was a mother and at least 3 children. The Mother gave commands to the players one at a time. Say, for example, "Linda, you may take one step forward." The player responds by asking, "Mother, may I?" If the player moves without requesting and obtaining permission, she is out of the game. The last remaining player wins the game.

We can learn a couple things from this simple game. First, permission to behave is required. Whether or not it is legal, what we do has to be sanctioned. And secondly, our thoughts sanction our behavior. Now note this, God or Satan sanctions all thought. Yes, we choose what we will think. But we do not decide the pool of thoughts from which

102

we choose a thought to think. Nor do we determine the depth or height of depravity or goodness of any one thought! We simply choose what we will think and thereby give life to behavior.

Behavior does not have a life of its own. It takes life and shape from our thoughts. In other words, what we think gives life and shape to our behavior. Proverbs 23:7 reads: "For as he thinks in his heart, so is he."

Sometimes we can look at our spouse's behavior and make an intelligent guess as to what he or she is thinking. At other times we cannot. However, at all times prayer and a heart filled with love and compassion are necessary to understand "why" our spouse behaves the way he or she does. Ecko was not content to know what I thought or felt about a matter, she desired to understand why. It is easy to make assumptions and even draw conclusions about our spouse. And when their behavior offends us, we naturally assume the worst of their thoughts. Love is not required for this. And when those behaviors are repetitive and impact us negatively, we seldom display the composure necessary to even try to understand. The Bible says in Proverbs 24:10:

> If you faint in the day of adversity, your strength is small.

Behavior draws on the thought life within us. It takes opportunity from our thoughts. Behavior is dependent on what we think and how we feel. You decide what you think and then you pick behavior that matches your thoughts. All that we see in self and others originates from what is not readily observable. Out of heart thoughts behavior proceeds.

Read Matthew 12:34:

> You offspring of vipers! How can you speak good things when you are evil [wicked]? For out of the fullness [the overflow, the superabundance] of the heart the mouth speaks.

103

And consider Luke 6:45:

> The upright [honorable, intrinsically good] man out of the good treasure [stored] in his heart produces what is upright [honorable and intrinsically good], and the evil man out of the evil storehouse brings forth that which is depraved [wicked and intrinsically evil]; for out of the abundance [overflow] of the heart his mouth speaks.

Matthew and Luke are saying that it is our heart that provides meaning for our words and ultimately gives life to our behavior. So as husbands and wives, one of our greatest challenges will be to see beyond what our spouse is actually doing, to the heart of the matter. Paul offers us some help in I Corinthians 4:16 - 18:

> Therefore we do not become discouraged [utterly spiritless, exhausted, and wearied out through fear]. Though our outer man is [progressively] decaying and wasting away, yet our inner self is being [progressively] renewed day after day. For our light, momentary affliction [this slight distress of the passing hour] is ever more and more abundantly preparing and producing and achieving for us an everlasting weight of glory [beyond all measure, excessively surpassing all comparisons and all calculations, a vast and transcendent glory and blessedness never to cease!], *since we consider and look not to the things that are seen but to the things that are unseen; for the things that are visible are temporal [brief and fleeting], but the things that are invisible are deathless and everlasting.*

Paul began Chapter four by alluding to the trials they had suffered. Read what Paul said beginning in verse 1:

> Since God has so generously let us in on what he is doing, we're not about to throw up our hands and walk off the job just because we run into occasional hard times. We refuse to wear masks and play games. We don't maneuver and manipulate behind the scenes. And we don't twist God's Word to suit ourselves. Rather, we keep everything we do and say out in the open, the whole truth on display, so that those who want to can

see and judge for themselves in the presence of God. ("The Message")

Understanding Is The Key

Paul tells us that understanding is one of the keys to not throwing in the towel, but is understanding. Herein lies the purpose of this book: to inspire understanding so that you don't throw in the towel on your marriage and renew your faith and hope that God can (with your cooperation) turn things around for the better of all!

Not only does Paul encourage us to stay in it, but this time with passionate refusal to wear disguises, cover our real needs and hold our spouse hostage. Today, we accept responsibility for our real needs and place them before God. And according to Philippians 4:19, He will supply all of our needs out of His treasury.

Forgiveness is about taking our stake out of the outcome so that we can fully participate with God's income. Now we don't know about you, but we would much rather receive income than incur expense. When our spouse has to behave in a manner prescribed by us and things have to happen a certain way, then all of our thoughts, time and energy will be spent ensuring this happens. Control and manipulation become our bedfellows.

When we remove our stake out of the ground, two things happen. We are free to respond to God in the moment and our spouse is also free to respond to God in the moment. And from here anything is possible! The anxiety that accompanies the fear of the unknown is swallowed up in knowing that God is for us and there is no one that can be against us (Romans 8:31). Besides, Proverbs 21:1 says that the heart of the king is in His hand to turn it in whatever direction He chooses, bestowing favor on whomsoever He wills.

Now we can leave the post of guarding our own lives and take the risks associated with truly loving our spouse. Since God has us covered, we are free to cover our spouse. David encourages us in Psalms 91:

> You who sit down in the High God's presence, spend the night in Shaddai's shadow, say this: 'God, you're my refuge. I trust in You and I'm safe!' That's right—He rescues you from hidden traps, shields you from deadly hazards. His huge outstretched arms protect you—under them you're perfectly safe; His arms fend off all harm. Fear nothing—not wild wolves in the night, not flying arrows in the day, not disease that prowls through the darkness, not disaster that erupts at high noon. Even though others succumb all around, drop like flies right and left, no harm will even graze you. You'll stand untouched, watch it all from a distance, and watch the wicked turn into corpses. Yes, because God's your refuge, the High God your very own home, evil can't get close to you, harm can't get through the door. He ordered His angels to guard you wherever you go. 'If you stumble, they'll catch you, their job is to keep you from falling.' You'll walk unharmed among lions and snakes, and kick young lions and serpents from the path. 'If you'll hold on to Me for dear life,' says God, 'I'll get you out of any trouble. I'll give you the best of care if you'll only get to know and trust Me. Call Me and I'll answer, be at your side in bad times; I'll rescue you, then throw you a party. I'll give you a long life, give you a long drink of salvation!' ("The Message")

Getting To The Heart Of The Matter

How can we bestow the gift of freedom on our spouse when he or she is physically abusing or neglecting us?

Gerald routinely pushed and shoved Gina. However, one day Gerald became so angry that he punched Gina in the eye. She suffered a detached retina. He took her to the hospital apologizing the entire way. Gerald persuaded Gina not to press charges. They returned home, but Gina was growing tired of living in fear.

For the next few weeks everything was fine. Gerald continued to show his remorse with gifts and attention. But one evening after work, Gerald came home agitated. His responses were short and terse with Gina. She invited him to the table to eat, along with their son. Gerald constantly challenged his son from the way he sat in the chair, to how he held his fork, to the correct way to cut his meat. Needful to say, Gerald was intense with all. Upon reaching across the table for the ketchup, Gerald's son knocked over the water pitcher.

That was it! Gerald shot up out of his chair, grabbed his son and threw him to the floor in disapproval. When he would not get up upon request, Gerald hoisted his 8-year-old son up by the arm. Fearing Gerald would become more abusive, Gina intervened by directing her son to his room. This infuriated Gerald. He grabbed Gina and threw her down on the floor, calling her derogatory names. Gina managed to make it to the bathroom and lock the door. Remembering she had put her cell phone in her pocket, she took the first and most courageous step she could toward freedom. Gina called the police who came and removed Gerald from the home.

Saying "No" to bailing him out was the next monumental step she took. By calling the police and allowing the law to manage Gerald's behavior, she performed the most loving act possible, given the circumstances.

For the first time, Gina told Gerald he was free to swing his arms. They were his arms to do with what he willed, however, his freedom to swing his arms ends when they threaten or make contact that is harmful to her or her son. In essence, Gina said to Gerald, "Since you swing your arms and hurt me, I need to step out of range until you gain self-control."

Gina did not tell Gerald to stop swinging. She could not control his arms. She also realized that Gerald was not in control when he became abusive. Reasoning with Gerald was ineffective. Repeated discussions changed nothing. Gina did not divorce Gerald as many might, but rather recognized Gerald was out of control and needed help. Gina decided that the first step was to get out of the way. When out of the way, Gina could distinguish Gerald from the anger and rage that routinely overtook him. And now they had the benefit of the court system to help them both. The judge addressed Gerald's abusive behavior with a short prison sentence and mandatory anger management classes. This gave Gina the time, as well as the mental and emotional space needed to gain additional knowledge and skills to effectively interact with her husband. Today, Gerald and Gina remain married. Their home has remained abuse-free for the past 6 years. To top it off, God added another child.

What About Neglect?

"Her body is not her own. She always says no and never initiates sex." Eric told us he felt Lisa deprived him of sex. He quoted I Corinthians 7:3 - 5:

> Let the husband render to his wife the affection due her, and likewise also the wife to her husband. The wife does not have authority over her own body, but the husband *does*. And likewise the husband does not have authority over his own body, but the wife *does*. *Do not deprive one another* except with consent for a time, that you may give yourselves to fasting and prayer; and come together again so that Satan does not tempt you because of your lack of self-control.

Eric felt justified in his anger toward Lisa. He got married to keep from sexual sin and now that he was married all he could think about was sexual sin. Eric blamed his wife's lack of responsiveness to his sexual desires. He was tired of her occasional sexual favors that have 'hurry up and finish' written all over them. He was certain he could find a woman that would appreciate his sexual desire.

But Eric is a Christian and desires to save his marriage. He also has already overcome pornography by walking with Christ. Eric loves Lisa and desires her physically. However, through counseling, he has realized she has a will of her own that must be honored. Eric feels neglected sexually.

But instead of taking matters into his own hands via masturbation or committing adultery, Eric decided to call on the same God that delivered him from pornography a few years earlier. He prayed with us for strength to sustain him through temptation and for the grace to decline sexual favors from his wife. I, (Tony) suggested he read and meditate on Matthew 19:12:

> For there are eunuchs who were born thus from *their* mother's womb, and there are eunuchs who were made eunuchs by men, and there are eunuchs who have made themselves eunuchs for the kingdom of heaven's sake. He who is able to accept *it,* let him accept *it.*

Through prayer and calling on the Lord, Eric decided that his response to Lisa neglecting him sexually would be to become a eunuch. He would make himself a eunuch for the kingdom of heaven's sake. Unbelievable—especially in this day and time! A man (or woman) that would choose to abstain from sex in the context of a sexually charged and permissible world; lacking in sexual restraint and selling everything from cars, to food, to people using sex is virtually unheard of—even in the Church! And when we factor into the equation that Eric is married, in the God ordained relationship biblically and officially designated sexual fulfillment and thereby entitled to sex more than any; his decision is absolutely absurd (and unexplainable) to the carnal mind!

Eric and I developed a strategy based on Matthew 19:12. Eric resolved to decline any and all sexual favors from Lisa. He desired more than her body—he desired Lisa.

Upon feeling aroused, Eric would read and pray Matthew 19:12 asking God for strength and grace in time of temptation. Eric would keep a journal, as he would use this to cultivate the fruit of self-control found in Galatians 5. Eric was also determined to treat Lisa as if she were satisfying him beyond his wildest imagination. No, it obviously did not feel that way, but the thought led to godly behavior toward her.

So weekly, Eric would meet with me to pray, discuss journal entries about the process of learning self-control, evaluate and adjust the plan accordingly. Eric accepted loving accountability and allowed God to fill the sexual void with love and self-control. Unbeknown to Eric at the time, his commitment to God's approach made him sexually desirable and eventually irresistible to Lisa.

Eric's self-control aroused Lisa. It broke through the denial of her God-given desire for sexual fulfillment, by sexually pleasing her husband. To say it another way, Eric's sexual restraint gave license and opportunity to God to stimulate and revive Lisa's sexual appetite. Eric was taking back what the enemy had stolen from Lisa through sexual molestation—the freedom to enjoy her sexuality with him!

By becoming a eunuch in marriage, Eric began realizing just how much sex and the thought of sex dominated his life. To him, sex was not an overflow of loving and caring for another deeply and intimately (in marriage as God ordained), but rather simply a means to self-gratification.

He admitted to a notorious sexual history. He told us of countless women left in the wake of his insatiable sexual appetite! Eric's remorse was that many of them too would become another's wife. And knowing what another's lack of sexual restraint had done to his wife, he could only imagine what he had done to another's wife. Then a friend showed Eric this scripture:

> For this is the will of God, your sanctification: that you should abstain from sexual immorality; that each of you should know how to possess his own vessel in sanctification and honor, not in passion of lust, like the Gentiles who do not know God; that no one should take advantage of and defraud his brother in this matter, because the Lord *is* the avenger of all such, as we also forewarned you and testified. For God did not call us to uncleanness, but in holiness. Therefore he who rejects *this* does not reject man, but God, who has also given us His Holy Spirit. (I Thessalonians 4:3-7)

Through all, Eric discovered the meaning of God's Word being a double-edged sword. For while God graced him to become a eunuch for Lisa's benefit, it was also making him holy, that is separated and pleasing to the Lord sexually. It was as much for him as it was for Lisa!

> But the fruit of the Spirit is love, joy, peace, longsuffering, kindness, goodness, faithfulness, gentleness, self-control. Against such there is no law. (Galatians 5:22, 23)

Christian, we have been spared judgment, *in order* that we might escape pride and lust that is in the world. These things ought not be named among us that profess to know Christ.

> But also for this very reason, giving all diligence, add to your faith virtue, to virtue knowledge, to knowledge self-control, to self-control perseverance, to perseverance godliness, to godliness brotherly kindness, and to brotherly kindness love. For if these things are yours and abound, *you will be* neither barren nor unfruitful in the knowledge of our Lord Jesus Christ.

A decision to abstain whether from sex, food, or any other thing that dominates us, must also validate the right of others to behave, as they will. This is love at its best!

Eric becoming a eunuch for the Kingdom's sake, afforded Lisa the freedom to behave as she willed. In the absence of threat of divorce, criticisms about her sexuality and steady love, Lisa experienced safety. Eventually, she took the risk to examine this area of her life with God and her husband. Their time spent talking soon turned to lovemaking and lovemaking to more talking and more talking to more lovemaking. They were full of love and their marriage became replete with sexual expression.

Freedom Costs

Eric's gift to Lisa was boundaries. By exercising sexual self-control and not accepting sexual favors, Eric conveyed his disapproval of sex on any terms. Unless Lisa was willing to participate fully with him in lovemaking, he would have none of it. Eric's ravenous sexual appetite made his decision to abstain from sex huge. And it made an incredible statement to Lisa. Lisa got the message that Eric loved her and because he loved her, he chose her and because he chose her, he wanted her and was willing to wait for all of her. Ultimately, they both got what they desired! Eric got more sex. Lisa got the feeling of being chosen for her person, rather than simply for her body!

Remember Gerald and Gina? Gerald's freedom cost Gina her silence and fear of reprisal. She confronted Gerald by taking a stand against abuse. Lisa's freedom cost Eric his God authorized right to sex (with his wife). Each was willing to pay the price to gain freedom for his and her spouse. Both recognized a gift each could offer toward this end. But it would be offered at the expense of what each learned to covet.

Gina coveted provision received from Gerald. Her life was infinitely better off materially with him than without him. Gina knew she could not live nearly as well without him as she could with him. At the risk of forfeiting a very comfortable lifestyle, Gina established boundaries. And these new boundaries were a gift to Gerald, albeit undesired, unappreciated and condemned at the time given. The first boundary was calling the police and allowing law enforcement to manage Gerald's behavior. It was the necessary help Gerald needed to face his rage and abusiveness.

Eric coveted sex. Foregoing sex and at the risk of not being sexually chosen by Lisa, Eric developed self-control. Abstaining from sex altogether until such time that Lisa desired and actively pursued him was very costly to a man dominated by sex. Eric had to wrestle with his worth, his manhood and his unabated desire for sexual fulfillment. But he would do so and with surprising results. Sexual self-restraint from one she loved was the gift Lisa required to be restored sexual wholeness. Only this gift, and from a loved one could overthrow the aftermath of Lisa's self-destructive thoughts and feelings that followed her older brother's lack of sexual restraint toward her.

Eric and Gina's gift to their respective spouses was priceless. They were the only ones that could only deliver these gifts. Prayer and encouragement from a group of well-informed Christians would benefit them greatly. Neither denied a desire for what each coveted. They offered themselves to God in spite of these belligerent, yelling and screaming desires that competed ruthlessly for their service. They identified with Jesus in the Garden of Gethsemane and discovered the reality of John 15: 13:

> Greater love has no one than this, that he lay down his life for his friends.

The day they made the decision to offer God their desires and rights, risking loss and deprivation is the day they became a friend to their respective spouse. It was also the day in which God turned the tide to their favor!

Freedom to choose is the most valuable asset we have as human beings. To deprive a spouse this basic right is to enslave them. The full beauty and value of a person can only be known when they are free to choose who they will be. We learn and change when we are permitted to be who we are in a safe place. And when that which we are not confronts who we are, only then do we have a choice about who we will be going forward.

Until then, all are slaves. We are imprisoned by experiences that validate the lies we believe about self and our spouse. And as long as we are not free, we can free no one else! This includes our spouse. Preventing our spouse from being who they are, through whatever method of control we exert, will breed contempt. Whenever compliance is forced whether passively or aggressively, we provoke our spouse to anger. Giving our spouse the gift of freedom enables us to see what's really going on.

Beneath The Surface

In the New International Version, Proverbs 20:5 reads:

> The purposes of a man's heart are deep waters, but a man of understanding draws them out.

All behavior has a reason. It is easy to attribute our behavior to others.

In the previous chapter, John blamed Brenda for his adulterous behavior. Brenda encouraged this by blaming herself. Neither was right. The reason John committed

114

adultery was far deeper. Brenda may have made it easier, but if it were not in John to commit adultery, he could not have been tempted! The reason John committed adultery rests within him like deep waters. He may not even understand why.

Understanding this about our spouse's hurtful behavior, knowing how to draw out our spouse's reason for such behavior and giving opportunities to reconcile his or her reason with truth, can happen only when we first pay the price for his or her freedom. When we pay for something we tend to value it differently. We also treat more kindly than we might otherwise. Valuing our spouse leads to more compassionate actions on our part. Still, sometimes we are not the best ones to draw out the reasons for our spouse's behavior. Counseling, classes and pastoral intervention may be appropriate.

In The Meantime

We can give our spouse the taste of freedom that that accompanies unconditional love. They will never be able to desire a love they have not felt. You must touch them. They cannot accept a love they cannot see. You must show them. They cannot speak of a love they have not heard. You must tell them. They cannot return a love they have not been given. You must give to them. And we must learn to do this in presence of our hurt, in face of our fear, without expecting anything from our spouse in return. Why would any do this? For one reason and one reason only: Christ did it for us! We please God by following Christ. And the rewards laid up for us in heaven will be determined by how well we have followed our Savior and Lord in spirit, mind and body! Consider Romans 5:8 again:

> But God shows and clearly proves His [own] love for us by the fact that while we were still sinners, Christ (the Messiah, the Anointed One) died for us. (Amplified Version)

This was the rationale for Paul's statement in Romans 12: 1, 2:

> I APPEAL to you therefore, brethren, and beg of you in view of [all] the mercies of God, to make a decisive dedication of your bodies [presenting all your members and faculties] as a living sacrifice, holy (devoted, consecrated) and well pleasing to God, which is your reasonable (rational, intelligent) service and spiritual worship. Do not be conformed to this world (this age), [fashioned after and adapted to its external, superficial customs], but be transformed (changed) by the [entire] renewal of your mind [by its new ideals and its new attitude], so that you may prove [for yourselves] what is the good and acceptable and perfect will of God, even the thing which is good and acceptable and perfect [in His sight for you].

These faith inspired actions, born out of sacrificial love are central to turning our spouses' hearts to God and us. When combined with the willingness to own our contribution to marital conflict, we offer God the best opportunity to bring about favorable and long-term changes in our marriage relationship.

During this process, God may give us understanding about why our spouse behaves the way he or she does. When He does, it is usually because He desires us to pray and develop compassion when we see our spouse in bondage. But typically, we do not. Oftentimes we use our understanding to crucify our spouse. Then they must not only overcome their own reasons for behaving as they do, but our criticism as well. When we do not hold our peace when appropriate, we only make it harder for our spouse. Author, Paul Eldridge, writes:

> Man is ready to die for an idea, provided that idea is not quite clear to him.

It is easy to profess love for someone we don't really know. However, it is quite another thing to proclaim our love for someone we do know and especially when that knowledge is unfavorable.

While dating and even through the beginning of marriage, we express a willingness to die for the one we love. Some have given up tremendous opportunities, lavish lifestyles and family inheritances for the one they love. And these early concessions serve as proof of our willingness to lay down our lives.

But somehow none of this prepares us for the ultimate request of marriage and that is to give up the way we think and feel—our reasons and our reality. To understand our spouses' reality we will have to abandon our own for a little while. Remember, their reality is just as real to them as ours is to us. It makes as much sense to them as ours does to us. And since they are often incompatible, we will have to let go of our own to understand and appreciate theirs! No way! That's just too much to ask! After all, we have already suffered indescribable pain at the hands of our spouse. It is one thing to experience pain by consent and quite another without consent. Marriage makes it painfully clear to us that if we desire our spouse to experience new life, then it is ours we must offer. Unfortunately, at least one out of two couples declines this lofty invitation.

> For people will be lovers of self and [utterly] self-centered, lovers of money and aroused by an inordinate [greedy] desire for wealth, proud and arrogant and contemptuous boasters. They will be abusive [blasphemous, scoffing], disobedient to parents, ungrateful, unholy and profane. (II Timothy 3:2)

Verse four tells us that men will be lovers of pleasure rather than lovers of God. Marriage is a true acid test revealing who and what we love. God demonstrated His love to us while we were practicing sin (Romans 5:8). And when Christ accomplished our freedom through the cross, He invited us to come as we are—dirty and defiled by sin. He did not say, "Get your 'self' cleaned up, put on your Sunday best and come to Me!"

If we could do this for our 'self,' the cross would be unnecessary. Yet, we desire our spouse to come correct, be correct and when they do hurt us, we demand they provide us proof they will never hurt us again. So are you saying that we should allow our spouse the freedom to do whatever they desire to our detriment and that of our children?

Giving Your Spouse Permission

Wait a minute! We were with you up until now! Are you saying that we should give our spouse permission to use household funds to support his or her addiction? No! The word permission is made up of two words: per and mission. The word, "per" means according to. The word "mission" means an aim or objective. When drugs and alcohol enslave a spouse, it becomes their mission to secure these things, oftentimes by any means necessary. Paul writes this about himself in Romans 7:14 - 16:

> Yes. I'm full of myself—after all, I've spent a long time in sin's prison. What I don't understand about myself is that I decide one way, but then I act another, doing things I absolutely despise. So if I can't be trusted to figure out what is best for myself and then do it, it becomes obvious that God's command is necessary. ("The Message")

Bondage is the inability to do what one desires and compulsion to do what one does not desire. As with any other sin, when a spouse is bound by drugs or alcohol, he or she is not in control. The courts appoint legal guardians upon ruling persons incompetent. In the same way, Christians married to spouses in bondage and unable to execute decisions resulting in their wellbeing, have spiritual guardians. Similarly, when a spouses' bondage threatens the health and safety of their family, they too will require a guardian. True guardians, both legal and spiritual have at heart the best interest of the one for whom they advocate. Notwithstanding that will consider all when making decisions on their behalf. Though we must caution you, managing your own interests while trying to represent your spouse's interests invites question of your motives. This is why husbands and wives need an extraordinary support team on the sidelines. A team of trusted people that can enter and offer help at any time. Your team might include your pastor, a counselor or therapist, an addictions support group, a mature Christian that may have overcome what you are facing and trusted, willing to tell you the truth friends!

Giving permission and supporting sinful behavior are not the same. When a spouse is rendered incompetent due to drugs, alcohol or any other acute or long-term condition, giving permission to manage family resources places all in jeopardy. In these kinds of situations, a spouse is wise to seek the counsel of a pastor, professional or trusted friend.

In most cases, giving our spouse permission does not involve substantial risks to the health and well-being of the family. However, this does not mean that our spouse's decisions will not hurt us. There are times when our spouse's behavior will hurt us, deeply, and yet not result in life-altering maladies. And while it may feel like it, the mark of true Christianity is found in thanking God for all things and receiving the truth each experience offers us. When we retaliate, we forfeit this nugget of truth and are subject to repeating the experience. Such repetition might be viewed as the loving gesture of a God and Father that does not want to see us fail. Understanding that all things are intended to bring us to God and ultimately work together for our good, also means that whatever happens to us, God can and will use it to bring us to His pre-determined end. He has a purpose for each life He creates.

The truth is, we are not really in control. While we may influence others, they maintain responsibility for how they choose to respond. Granting our spouse permission is both an admission that we do not have control over him or her and an affirmation of free will. Giving our spouse the freedom to choose how he or she will live, even to our own hurt, is the greatest act of love we can offer. We may feel powerless in this, yet it is the very nature of love.

Love Without Conditions

God loves us. He values free will. So, He allows us to make choices. God doesn't always protect us from the decisions we make that result in our harm, or others for that matter. He loves us enough to grant us everything we need in order to realize who we perceive our "self" to be—right or wrong, pleasing or displeasing. He extends the same to our spouses. God does this knowing they will hurt us and we them. And yet, He allows it. Why? God Almighty is so supremely confident in His Son and the Holy Spirit's ability to use all to our benefit and especially so when we are willing. It is His Sovereignty: His absolute authority and power over everything and in everything and the wherewithal to stop it, change it and use it at any given time that He permits all.

God loves us through His own hurt. Loving God's way is not without opposition. Our spouse won't roll over, play nice and indulge our unconvincing attempts at love. In fact, it is their opposition that both proves and establishes the love of God in us. Matthew and Paul concur that it is necessary that opposition come to distinguish what is of God and what is not.

We invite those we may unknowingly need into our lives to realize who we are and who we are not. If we believe we are forgiving, then we invite people into our lives that need forgiving. After all, if we believe we have it, why shouldn't

120

God send those that are in need of it? And when they come, why shouldn't our spouse be among them, if not in front of them? When we find that our responses are not forgiving, then we must re-evaluate what we believe about our "self." If we do not, we risk believing a lie and the truth cannot help us.

If we believe we love, then we invite those into our lives that need love. Mostly, these people show up unloving, hostile and in denial. And if it pleases God to send our spouse ahead of them, who are we to argue? Our spouse needs love and forgiveness and the freedom that accompanies it to have an opportunity to grow and change. We are our brothers' and sisters' keepers. We have been given the power to set our brother or sister free, especially when that brother or sister is our spouse.

I Corinthians 7:14 says:

> For the unbelieving husband is sanctified by the wife, and the unbelieving wife is sanctified by the husband; otherwise your children would be unclean, but now they are holy.

We have the power to influence our spouse to change. Paul said of Jesus in Hebrews 2:11:

> For both He who sanctifies and those who are being sanctified *are* all of one, for which reason He is not ashamed to call them brethren...

CHAPTER 10
YOU'VE GOT THE POWER!
"When we change, everything in relationship with us must change!"

GROWTH AND CHANGE are inevitable! They will occur. We will either become abnormally hard and stiff in wrong thinking accompanied by rigid inflexible attitudes and behaviors; or we will become pliable and teachable. The result of the latter is a changed mind, acceptance of godly attitudes and new behaviors to go along with it. Either way, we will change by becoming more of what we already are, or something entirely new and different. Langston Hughes wrote, "Growth is impossible without change and he who cannot change his mind cannot change anything."

Paul wrote it this way in Romans 12:2:

> Do not be conformed to this world [this age], [fashioned after and adapted to its external, superficial customs], but be transformed [changed] by the [entire] renewal of your mind [by its new ideals and its new attitude], so that you may prove [for yourselves] what is the good and acceptable and perfect will of God, even the thing which is good and acceptable and perfect [in His sight for you]. (Amplified Version)

Eugene Petersen in "The Message" includes verse one and writes it this way:

> So here's what I want you to do, God helping you: Take your everyday, ordinary life—your sleeping, eating, going-to-work, and walking-around life—and place it before God as an offering. Embracing what God does for you is the best thing you can do for him. Don't become so well adjusted to your culture that you fit into it without even thinking. Instead, fix your attention on God. You'll be changed from the inside out. Readily recognize what he wants from you, and quickly respond to it. Unlike the culture around you, always dragging you down to its level of immaturity, God brings the best out of you, develops well-formed maturity in you.

We Will Change

Clearly, God requires that we change. Therefore, not only must we change, we will change. It's the law. It's God's law. It's unbreakable. This is why we can marry and remarry and still the same challenges confront us. Our spouse is not our problem! We need to change. Changing partners does not change the lesson God would have us to learn. Consider Philippians 1:6:

> And I am convinced and sure of this very thing, that He Who began a good work in you will continue until the day of Jesus Christ [right up to the time of His return], developing [that good work] and perfecting and bringing it to full completion in you. (Amplified Version)

And just what is full completion? Let's return to God's original intention: a family in His image. Reread Romans 8:29:

> For those whom He foreknew [of whom He was aware and loved beforehand], He also destined from the beginning [foreordaining them] to be molded into the image of His Son [and share inwardly His likeness], that He might become the firstborn among many brethren. (Amplified Version)

Verse 29 says that we were called according to His purpose and plan. God will not be denied. He created us. We did not create ourselves. Moreover, those that profess being in relationship with Christ have been bought with a price and their life is no longer their own to do with what they will. For this reason, we can be assured that God is at work in all things, fitting them together for our good and His glory.

Paul prefaces our selection by establishing God's intention in allowing good as well as harm to come to us:

... all things work together for good to those who love God, to those who are the called according to *His* purpose." (Romans 8:28)

While all that our spouse does to us is not good, God assures us that He will work it together for our good because He chose us to be conformed to His image. We can take comfort in knowing that what was intended for evil, God uses to benefit us and bring glory to Himself.

People change when they hurt enough, get fed up enough and/or get tired enough! Generally, this means we must be provoked to change. Sometimes this takes many years, which explains the phenomena of couples choosing divorce after twenty plus years of marriage!

Most of us do not live with the mindset of change. Rather, human nature clearly looks to fossilize good and pleasurable experiences and eradicate the painful ones. We live our lives avoiding pain and pursuing pleasure. But it is the pain we avoid that comes to expose our true thoughts and feelings. And until we can be honest about our "self," a hope and a prayer will not change us.

Recently, I (Kim) realized that I did not understand the reason for the adversarial tone I sometimes used with my husband. For years, I attributed it to something Tony did. When he stopped whatever it was, I was fine and thus thought no more of my own agitation. After all, it only surfaced when Tony did something that threatened my wellbeing. Therefore, I had no reason to inquire further, or so I thought.

But as years went on, this agitation surfaced more regularly. It looked like impatience, a preference to be alone and emotionally detached. While I grew to the place of admitting these unlovely sinful behaviors, I still did not know why I felt such hostility. This began a whole new phase of my journey with Christ. I did not desire to be angry, but felt powerless to change it and the growing distance between Tony and me. I felt like a hypocrite— behaving one way with my husband and differently with others. It was a discrepancy of growing proportions. I could not reconcile it in my own mind, so I began to ask God why I felt and behaved the way I did with my husband.

I had lost admiration, emotional love and desire for my husband. And as "marriage experts," we were not headed in the right direction. Moreover, to whom do the experts talk to in order to gain clarity? I felt alone. So, I spent more and more time in prayer—humbling my "self" by praying and seeking His face, and inquiring of God concerning my lot.

I will not tell you that it was easy and that God rushed to me with wisdom and insight. And I don't believe that He wouldn't or even couldn't, but so much of the work required of us involves coming to grips with the unlovely parts of "self." Human nature naturally declines such invitations and the self-proclaimed "godly" feel such work is beneath them. So you can see the challenge God has in helping us.

But He did help me and continues to help me. One of the things I learned is that I (naturally) have an "independent" mentality or spirit, if you like. For a long time, I honestly thought this was a good thing. I was self-motivated and self-reliant—able to begin and finish things on my own. I didn't need anyone, especially one that threatened my wellbeing. Don't get me wrong, I could and often did choose to join my husband at various times and purposes—I just was not able to sustain such connection. When the project or purpose was over the need to be connected was also over. Projects and purposes kept us connected. But I had never learned how to connect spiritually or emotionally for any sustained period of time with anyone!

And then there are the opposing forces to marriage. God's enemies benefit from divided homes and hearts—mine included! I Peter 5:8 reads:

> Be sober, be vigilant; because your adversary the devil walks about like a roaring lion, seeking whom he may devour.

Jesus adds this in Luke 22:31:

> And the Lord said, 'Simon, Simon! Indeed, Satan has asked for you, that he may sift *you* as wheat. But I have prayed for you, that your faith should not fail; and when you have returned to *Me,* strengthen your brethren.'

Embracing The Truth

As I embraced the truth about my "self," understanding the real reasons for my behavior became easier to accept also. I was raised to be independent. My mother, grandmother, great-grandmother all contributed to the lessons I learned. Upon careful search, my instructor went as far back as Eve—the mother of all living. And all these lessons were watered by slavery and fed by the feminist movement. While this book is about neither, it is interesting to consider that both taught us how to raise responsible, self-sufficient daughters, while ignoring our sons. Herein, lies our work if we are to restore marriage to the Church as God intends.

Eve used free will to choose what she perceived to be in her best interest. Not only did this constitute an act of independence, it also blatantly disregarded God's authority. In other words, unlike Jesus, Eve used her God–given freewill in a manner that was inconsistent with God's authority and protection. By doing so, Eve was irreverent! She was independent and irreverent. Jesus was independent and yet reverent. Read how Jesus responded to the devil in Matthew 4:8 - 9:

For the third test, the Devil took him to the peak of a huge mountain. He gestured expansively, pointing out all the earth's kingdoms, how glorious they all were. Then he said, 'They're yours—lock, stock, and barrel. Just go down on your knees and worship me, and they're yours. Jesus' refusal was curt: 'Beat it, Satan!' He backed his rebuke with a third quotation from Deuteronomy: 'Worship the Lord your God, and only Him. Serve Him with absolute single-heartedness.' ("The Message")

Jesus honored His Father with His God-given free will. Eve honored herself with her God-given free will. Like Eve, I (Kim) was honoring my "self" with my God-given ability to choose for my "self." Jesus was reverent—He never once questioned who God was. On one occasion, Jesus told Pilate that he could have no authority over Him unless His Father had given it to Him. So Jesus didn't even question who Pilate was. He accepted Pilate's placement in His life as Divine.

On the other hand, Eve was irreverent. She questioned God's authority, that is, who He was (to her). In Isaiah 14:13 and 14, we discover that Satan also challenged God's authority, that is, who God was (to him). Read it for yourselves:

You said to yourself, 'I'll climb to heaven. I'll set my throne over the stars of God. I'll run the assembly of angels that meets on sacred Mount Zion. I'll climb to the top of the clouds. I'll take over as King of the Universe!' ("The Message")

Satan did not simply question God's behavior, but challenged God's authority. This is the difference between questioning what someone does versus who someone is? Now how does it look for creation to challenge the Creator? And yet, Eve did just that. She challenged God and Adam. So did I. I opposed God.

I opposed my husband. I used my freedom to challenge what Tony did. I debated his opinions, question his

128

decisions, criticized his solutions, amplified his mistakes and literally found fault with almost everything he did that did not include or benefit me! But even more grievous to God was questioning my husband's position as one in authority over me. Truthfully, I resented his authority and so I questioned his competency to lead.

Practically, this looked like promoting our equality. I asserted my individual rights, especially when I disagreed with him. I demanded my opinion be noted and reflected in all he did. I nurtured feelings of superiority that erupted whenever we discussed anything intellectual or spiritual. I thought I knew more in most cases and as much in the remainder of cases as Tony. We were a marriage of equals! We were partners. This is what we were to lead to believe. We were told this by well intentioned, albeit misinformed professionals and clergy. If so, then why did I feel I had to fight so hard to be what they said we were?

Later we learned that God didn't see it that way at all! We were not equal. We were not partners in marriage. Although God created us equal, He did not position us equally as husband and wife. Tony was given authority to take responsibility for me. I was given power to become responsive to him. God gave Tony permission and placement from which to assume responsibility for me; and the work assigned to us.

On the other hand, God gave me the ability to respond to Tony and to ensure the work assigned us was accomplished! Without the right or permission to do something, we behave illegally. And without the ability to do something, we are lame. Both are required. Neither is optional. We must have both authority and power. All relationships are based on this principle and truth. In marriage, husband and wife though not equal are equally required. Together they bring both the right and ability to change those to whom they have been assigned!

I have had to ask my husband to forgive me many, many times. And I still do! Don't worry, I haven't used up the "70 times 7, or even the 7 times in one day" quota (Matthew 18: 22 and Luke 17: 4)—so we're good! The bottom line is when left to my self, I sin against God and those I love and care about become collateral damage.

A word to husbands that are thinking about underscoring these words, highlighting the entire page, maybe even ripping the page out and putting it on your wife's pillow. Please understand. I was not intentionally trying to hurt my husband, as I am certain it sometimes appeared. I was trying to protect my self. It wasn't that I didn't love my husband. I simply love my self more.

Although I challenged my husband's authority, I sincerely believed I was helping him. And while nothing I have written would give the least discerning reader the impression I was helping, I was deceived. Until I could come to grips with my own hurt and fear, I could only see my behavior as helpful Tony at best and necessary by virtue of his faults.

Thank God my husband was able to get beyond my hardened, matter of fact exterior to the heart that was so desperately in need of love. God gave him the authority to do so. A husband's God-given authority when rightly used can do more to win the affection of their wives than all the gifts, words of affirmation, acts of service and quality time could ever do alone!

Embracing The Change

Rewind. You should know that it wasn't until I got sick and tired of being sick and tired that I even considered a change. At first, it was mostly about changes Tony could make. When that didn't work, I considered the external changes I could make—moving out, moving away. But I couldn't do these, so I did what I always did—emotionally and physically detach.

This was easy at first. I had always done this when I felt powerless in changing others. However, the longer I remained detached, the more painful it became. When I could no longer take the pain, and refused to mask it with shopping and food, I discovered the grace to cry out to God at the doorstep of my heart. I asked Him to change me: to heal my spirit that I might possess my thoughts and feelings. He answered me. And again I would like to be able to tell you that a miracle happened all in the matter of moments. But it did not. By crying out, a dialogue was initiated between God and me. We were on speaking terms about a very vulnerable area of my life. But we would need to connect for me to realize a change. I was willing: He was able.

Gradually, I began to change and develop a newfound love and admiration for Tony. I became sensitive to the presence and outcomes of my independence. I no longer wanted to offend God by being irreverent to Tony. As I have changed, Tony has become more and more supportive.

We Will Get Tired

Coming to the recognition that I needed to change wore me out! But then I realized we're supposed to get tired! To deny our tiredness and readiness to give up is to delay the coming to the end of "self" and our way of doing things. It is necessary that we come to the end of our "self" if we are to discover the grace of God. Grace begins when our ability ends. Consider how Paul encourages us a few verses before Romans 8:29:

> Meanwhile, the moment we get tired in the waiting, God's Spirit is right alongside helping us along. If we don't know how or what to pray, it doesn't matter. He does our praying in and for us, making prayer out of our wordless sighs, our aching groans. He knows us far better than we know ourselves, knows our pregnant condition, and keeps us present before God. That's why we can be so sure that every detail in our lives of love for God is worked into something good. (Romans 8:26-28, "The Message")

The difficulty with being tired is learning that there is still road that we must travel. And while rest is needful and provided, it does not alleviate the effort that still must be applied in order to change. Most of us have experienced the temporary results of changing our minds, without allowing God to change our hearts. Yet, only when our heart is healed and healthy are we capable of sustained change. Read Proverbs 18:14:

> The strong spirit of a man sustains him in bodily pain or trouble, but a weak and broken spirit who can raise up or bear? (Amplified Version)

A weak or wounded heart is incapable of maintaining thoughts and attitudes that precipitate change in us and influence change in our spouse. Rest is necessary. But if we rest and do not seek healing and restoration for our soul, we will find our self languishing in the day of adversity.

> If you faint in the day of adversity, your strength is small. (Proverbs 24:10, Amplified Version)

Whenever we suffer hurt by the hand of another, we need healing. In no relationship is the need for healing more evident than in marriage. Attempting to fix behavior without allowing God to fix our heart is futile.

Jeremiah was challenged by perpetual pain. On one occasion, he asked God the reason for this. God responded in Jeremiah 15:18 - 20.

> Why is my pain perpetual and my wound incurable, refusing to be healed? Will you indeed be to me like a deceitful brook, like waters that fail and are uncertain? Therefore thus says the Lord [to Jeremiah]: If you return [and give up this mistaken tone of distrust and despair], then I will give you again a settled place of quiet and safety, and you will be My minister; and if you separate the precious from the vile [cleansing your own heart from unworthy and unwarranted suspicions concerning God's faithfulness], you shall be My mouthpiece. [But do not yield to them.] Let them return to you--not you to [the people]. And I will make you to this people a fortified, bronze wall; they will fight against you, but they will not prevail over you, for I am with you to save and deliver you, says the Lord. (Amplified Version)

Notice Jeremiah asked God about his own pain. God talked to Jeremiah about how to resolve his pain. God's instructions required something from Isaiah. Others were unable to relieve the source of Jeremiah's pain because it was internal. Jeremiah had a heart problem. No one could fix Jeremiah's heart except God. So God tells Jeremiah to return to Him and He will resolve the problem and thereby relieve the pain.

When we are tired, we need presence of mind to return to God so that we can be healed. In so many areas of our lives, we are like the prodigal son. Having gone astray, we must eventually return home to be healed.

We Will Overcome

God is committed to all who enter into marriage. He desires that we become a testimony of His grace as we undergo the change process. We are assured victory at the outset.

133

> For I know the plans I have for you, declares the LORD, plans to prosper you and not to harm you, plans to give you hope and a future. (Jeremiah 29:11, New International Version)

Not only so, but Isaiah 46:10 indicates that:

> I make known the end from the beginning, from ancient times, what is still to come. I say: My purpose will stand, and I will do all that I please. (New International Version)

God wants us to win! He is on our side encouraging us, training us and cheering us on. And He is for you and your husband or wife. So, then, who is it that can be against you. You can overcome an oppositional spouse by accepting God's grace, allowing Him to heal your heart and letting go of the thoughts and attitudes that got you here in the first place.

As we give our hearts to God and allow Him to heal and strengthen us, we are able to comprehend His love. We will be able to see it and recognize His love in people, places and things that the unloving and unforgiving cannot. The beauty and grace of love is not confined to the warm and fuzzy feelings exchanged between husband and wife. The beauty, grace and strength of real love is in laying down one's way of thinking and behaving for another. In John 15:13, Jesus said:

> No one has greater love [no one has shown stronger affection] than to lay down [give up] his own life for his friends. (Amplified Version)

Right now, your spouse may need a friend, more than a husband or a wife. Perhaps, God is asking you to be a friend that He may return to you a husband or a wife. He is faithful; you can trust Him.

CHAPTER 11
YOU'RE SUPPOSED TO WIN!

"If people can't see what GOD is doing, they stumble all over themselves: but when they attend to what He reveals, they are most blessed." (Proverbs 29:18) ("The Message")

WE CAN THINK of no more fitting way to end this book and for you to begin your new life with your spouse than by sharing renowned author, marriage proponent and family man, Gary Smalley's, experience with his wife Norma. Gary writes:

> When my wife stopped fighting me about my obsession toward work, as well as other issues, she unleashed a powerful force in my life, though neither of us understood it at the time. Independent of me, Norma learned how to get in line and bring her needs to God. Rather than complain to me, she prayed, 'Lord, thank you that all I need is you. You know I want a good relationship with Gary and that I want him to spend more time at home. You also know that I'm not very strong physically. I'm so tired that I don't feel I can last much longer under this strain. I'm coming to you with these requests because I know that if I need Gary at home, You can make it happen. Or you can take away my desire for him to be home. I'm going to stop fighting Gary and instead ask you either to change him or to meet my needs in some other way.'

> To find God's fulfillment, Norma took steps similar to those I later discovered. She stopped expecting life from me and started looking to God. She realized I not only would not, but could not, energize her life, so she went to the source of life and asked Him to energize her.

> The results were startling. I noticed the change almost immediately. When I came home from work, I sensed a calm spirit in our house. Norma's face was peaceful, no longer tense. Instead of the usual harsh words, her conversation was quiet and she was more interested in asking me how my day had gone than in relating her activities with the children.

> It was in that context that Norma talked to me about her need for help. A few days later, I couldn't keep from asking what had

happened. 'Gary, I got tired of fighting you,' she explained calmly. "I realized that I wasn't trusting God concerning our marriage and family, and so I decided to stop complaining and start praying. I've told God that I would like you to spend more time at home, and if I really need that, I know God will make the necessary changes.'

Imagine what that did to me. I was instantly convicted that my priorities were wrong. And that wasn't all. Because Norma had changed, I wanted to spend more time at home. That was the week I asked Bill to change my job so I could spend more time meeting my family's needs.

Norma stopped looking to (me) people, things, and her work, and turned instead to a trustworthy God who answers the persistent prayers of His children. God promises life -- and God delivers!" (Smalley Relationship Center 2002)

Norma Smalley discovered the true source of marital satisfaction— *trust and obey* God. Marital fulfillment is the by-product of one spouse yielding completely and wholeheartedly to God. So often we acknowledge God on our wedding day and try to manage the rest of our married life on our own. We ascribe lip service to God while the thing we hold most dear remains far from Him. We profess to know Him, as Paul tells Titus (1:16), but deny Him in the way we live and manage relationships. Somehow when we get into marriage and the unavoidable, inherent conflict, we forget that:

God *is* our refuge and strength, a very present help in trouble. (Psalm 46:1)

The Message Bible states it this way:

God is a safe place to hide, ready to help when we need him.

Verses two and three go on to read:

We stand fearless at the cliff-edge of doom, courageous in sea, storm and earthquake, before the rush and roar of oceans, the tremors that shift mountains.

Those that experience sustained conflict (and by the way, all of us have at one time or another) do not perceive God as present and ready to help. He tells us that if we lack wisdom, we can ask Him for it and He will give it to us without finding fault with us. When we ask for God's help, He does not criticize us and make us feel bad. Nor, does He disgrace us. But neither will He begin by focusing on our spouse. When we go to God for help, He is first and foremost concerned with us, our welfare and how we are responding to what is happening. Stephen Covey writes:

> Ten-percent of life is made up of what happens to you. Ninety-percent of life is decided by how you react. What does this mean? We really have no control over ten-percent of what happens to us. We cannot stop the car from breaking down. The plane will be late arriving, which throws our whole schedule off. A driver may cut us off in traffic. We have no control over this ten-percent. The other ninety-percent is different. You determine the other ninety-percent. How—by your reaction.

Our spouse has and will do things that directly and indirectly hurt us. Whether it is as simple as the tone of their voice or as complex as adultery resulting in a child, we will each have to manage the blows we are dealt. No level of admission or godly sorrow received from our spouse alters the internal work of learning how to love unconditionally.

God will not allow us to use our spouse, or anyone else for that matter, to justify our behavior. When we come to God, we must first believe that He is and that He is the rewarder of them that diligently seek Him. Christian, God loves us— you and me! As many of us know, one of the most frustrating experiences we can have is to desire more for our spouse than they do for themselves. Jim Carey, in the movie, "Bruce Almighty" conveys this frustration. Toward the end of the movie, he asked God (Morgan Freeman) how to get the woman he loved to realize and respond to his love without manipulating her in any way? Morgan Freeman responded telling Carey that he now understood His (God's) challenge! Any sort of manipulation diminishes the beauty of a man or woman willingly and freely choosing another. Therefore, we must continually renew our commitment to become who God would have us to be. By doing so, we become our utmost and highly desirable.

Don't Lift Another Finger For Your Spouse

You can significantly increase your desirability and you won't have to lift another finger for your spouse to do it! Sound impossible? To those who have resigned themselves to believe marriage is like a ball and chain, it is! But to those who thoroughly consider ideas presented in this book as they relate to God's Word, a whole new realm of possibility lies before you. And the best part is that you don't have to wait until experience brings you this revelation—you can meditate on these truths and allow God to bring you into experience. Norma Smalley discovered this and so did a woman I met several years ago.

Colette allowed God to change her while she waited on Him to change her husband Darryl. For twenty plus years Darryl ran the streets. Colette waited at home, always receiving Darryl when he came in from his escapades. She allowed God to teach her how to love him when he was unlovable to her naked eyes. Colette allowed God to use her husband's folly to reveal the true condition of her own heart.

And while it was easy to see her own goodness compared to his badness, Colette realized there was as much, if not more work to be accomplished in her own heart. This became her focus and work with God—to become the woman He intended. It paid off for Colette when Darryl finally came home for good! He was sorrowful for all the pain and suffering he caused his wife and vowed to change. Today, Darryl serves as a deacon in his local church and cherishes

Colette. His love for her is obvious to all. Only pain and suffering and unconditional love can produce such devotion to God and another.

Marriage Is Perfect

Marriage does exactly what it is designed to do. It is a vehicle that drives us to God. It is a machine that makes us one. It does all of this by design and on purpose. It is programmed with owner specifications to make men into husbands and women into wives; together bearing offspring, called the family of God. Albeit, each individual is unique, yet shares God's identity.

Marriage is perfect. It is a flawless method of providing a taste of the Divine Life, inspiration and provocation to grow and change.

Becoming one is no small task! And it seldom happens all at one time. Somebody has to go first. Becoming one means giving up and giving over our life—our way of thinking and behaving to God. When we do so, He gives us His mind and responses in exchange. As we discipline ourselves in this manner, the love of God has unobstructed passage to our spouse and love can begin to change our spouse into the person He created him or her to be. God's love is just that powerful!

Our Prayer For You

Our prayer for everyone who reads this book is that they will surrender their lives to the Lordship of Jesus Christ and accept marriage as one of the primary methods God offers for us to experience Him and be transformed by Him.

So we pray, 'Lord, may each person who reads this book lay down his or her own agenda of trying to change their spouse and release him or her into Your hands. Cause each one to examine his own heart in light of You, and You alone. Give to each one the spirit of wisdom and revelation in the knowledge of You, and open their eyes that they may comprehend Your love. Reveal to them what bountiful joy and peace await them that believe and enter this love. Grant them unprecedented grace to receive, be filled to overflowing and ultimately possessed by Your unconditional love. Finally, may they glorify You and be revealed to all by virtue of their love for one another.'

We encourage you to continue the paradigm shift in how you think and respond to marriage at www.radicallove.org.

HERE'S WHAT YOU CAN DO:

Share your response to the book, "Your Spouse Is Not Your Problem!"

Read what others are saying.

Post an insight that you incorporated into your relationship.

Communicate and interact with Tony and Kim.

Purchase additional gift copies, or copies for use in a small group.

Invite Tony and/or Kim to speak.

ADDITIONAL RESOURCES

Radical Love:
"Getting to the Heart of the Matter in Marriage!"
**a couples 12-week, faith-based marriage skills building program
for small group study**

Radical Love Home Study:
Self-Study Version

True Love:
"Falling In Love Is Easy, It's Staying There That's Hard!"
**a wives 8-week, faith-based knowledge and skill building
program for small group study**

Bold Love
"Help, I'm Married to a Strong Will Woman"
(Currently offered in seminar format only)

One Love:
"Planning a Life That Includes a Wedding Day!"
(Currently offered in seminar and retreat format only)

Radical Living:
**Free monthly e-newsletter
To subscribe go to www.radicallove.org**

For more information on scheduling authors, Tony and/or
Kim Moore to speak at your next event go to:

www.radicallove.org, call: 1-866-RADLOVE, or e-mail us at:
info@radicallove.org

About the Authors

Tony and Kim Moore have been married since 1986 and friends twice as long. Tony has a Bachelor's Degree in Business Administration from LaSalle University, located in Philadelphia, PA. He also holds a Doctorate in Ministry from Beacon University. Tony is a Licensed Pastoral Counselor and a Certified Sports Counselor and works with professional athletes and their spouses.

Kim holds a Bachelor's Degree in Psychology from Howard University, located in Washington, D.C. and Master's Degree in Social Work from Temple University, located in Philadelphia, PA. Kim is completing the requirements for a Doctorate in Ministry. She is a Licensed Christian Counselor.

Both are ordained ministers. In 2000, Tony and Kim founded the Center on Christian Relationships, Inc. (CCR) to restore trust and integrity to relationships through curriculum for small groups and individual study. CCR is presently the sole distributor of Radical Love and its related resources. In 2002, Tony Moore founded and now pastors Community of Faith Family Church in Buford, GA.

Tony and Kim have two daughters, born eight years and three days apart: Taylor Anastasia in March 1989 and Jordan Aliyia in March 1997. The Moore's have resided in metro Atlanta since 1994 with their daughters and 3 dogs—*miniature pinschers.*

The Moores enjoy motorcycles, water sports and especially relaxing in the Caribbean!